# How NOT *to be* broke

*A book about money, self-worth and how to leave a lasting legacy with your soloprenuer business.*

By

**JULIE CREFFIELD**

How NOT to be Broke

Published: 28th September 2023
Publisher: Julie Creffield



This book has been written as a guide for solopreneurs and small business owners but does not constitute financial advice. The book is not intended to be a source of financial or legal advice. Making adjustments to a financial strategy or plan should only be undertaken after consulting with a professional.

The publisher and the author make no guarantee of financial results obtained by using this book. The Author is not liable for any complications, investments, purchases, injuries, loss or medical problems arising from or in connection with using this book.

Thank you for respecting the hard work of this author.

Find out more about the author and upcoming books at www.juliecreffield.com or on Instagram @julie_creffield

To Rose, you make me the wealthiest
human that ever lived

# *TABLE OF CONTENTS*

# *FOREWORD*

***Alison Edgar MBE***

What do you want?

That's the million-dollar question in life AND in business.

If NOT being BROKE as a business owner is anywhere on that list, then you need to stop making excuses and start taking action today.

As an undiagnosed dyslexic growing up in a high rise flat in Clydebank, Scotland I left school at 16 with few qualifications, but big aspirations. In 2020 I received an MBE for recognition of my work with entrepreneurs, and in 2023 I made my TV debut on the Amazon Prime show Ready, Set, Start-up.

Now, I didn't get any of that from wishful thinking, I am a go-getter, I am tenacious, and I go after what it is I want. I'm not a believer in manifestation, even though I know Julie says this plays some part for her, but we both agree that wealth creation is a learned skill, and is ultimately about putting in the work.

I first met Julie back in 2013 when she was headlining The Festival of Female Entrepreneurs. We sat up in the hotel bar into the wee hours, talking all things sales, business, and running marathons.

I remember thinking,

*"this lady is going places"*

She smashed that talk, getting herself not one but two standing ovations from the audience of ambitious female business owners, and I knew even though she was just at the start of her entrepreneurial journey with her business Too Fat to Run, she would go on to do great things in business more generally.

She was on a mission. A mission to change the direction of her own life, while at the same time impacting the lives of others just like her. She had a fire in her belly, much like the fire in mine. I have followed the ups and downs of her career ever since.

I bet it would have been easy after being made redundant while 6 months pregnant and again a decade later after moving into her dream home, for her to be angry and bitter, but instead she used her challenging circumstances to her advantage and is now sharing the lessons in this book about the grit and determination needed to succeed as a solopreneur.

Having a vision is important, but you still need to grab opportunities with both hands, not just sit and wait for your goals, dreams and ideal income to come to you. Money doesn't grow on trees, it grows when you take action, and go after what you want.

And if anyone can teach you how to get on track financially and change your *"life is not fair"* narrative to one that really serves you it is Julie.

**Broke (adj.)** From obsolete past particle of break; extension to "insolvent" is first recorded in 1716 (broken in this sense is attested from 1590s). Old English cognate *broch* meant, in addition to "that which breaks" "affliction, misery"

# *THE HOW NOT TO BE BROKE GLOSSARY*

Words matter.

How we find them, how we use them, the power we give to them... but also how their meaning changes over time.

Our financial education and confidence to talk about money using the right words matters too, which is why this book is scattered with dictionary explanations and short snap shots of etymology...where words came from and how their meaning has changed.

Sometimes it's about re-educating ourselves, unlearning some of the more problematic beliefs or understandings about money that no longer serve us, and sometimes it's about peeking into brand new ideas and concepts and drawing a line under old-school ways of doing things.

Let's start with the word BROKE.

Firstly, you are NOT broke, you never have been, and you never will be again and I hereby banish you from using that phrase in relation to your wealth or self-value ever again...and here's why.

You can be financially challenged for sure, you can be facing difficult times...but never broke, because what's the opposite of Broke? It's not RICH, its Fixed... and as I said before you are not broken, and you do not need fixing... maybe it is the world that does.

Now we have that out of the way I thought it useful to kick things off with a little glossary to whet your appetite for all things financial literacy. Most glossaries can be found at the back of a book, but we are facing this head on from the get-go.

Are you ready?

A - Asset: A useful or valuable thing, person, or quality. In financial terms, it's something that has measurable value that can be converted into cash. It can however increase and decrease in value over time and can also be subjective. My boobs for example are often considered my best asset, whereas I would argue it's my humour and wit, especially as the latter are less likely to depreciate over time.

B - Budget: A financial plan for a defined period, often one year. It may also include planned sales volumes and revenues, resource quantities, costs, and expenses. The word can also be used to describe a low-cost option in the context of airlines, food items, ex boyfriends etc

C - Credit: The ability of a customer to obtain goods or services before payment, based on the trust that payment will be made in the future. Can be amassed over time. You can also be a credit to someone else, and other people can sometimes take credit for your hard work... we call those people wankers.

D - Dividend: A sum of money paid (typically annually, but often whenever a business owner thinks they can afford to) by a company to its shareholders out of its profits (or reserves). Something may or may not pay dividends later down the line.

E - Equity: The ownership interest of shareholders in a corporation. In the context of property, it's the difference between the property's market value and the homeowner's mortgage debt. This term can also be explored in relation to fairness, all things being equal.

F - Fixed Expenses: Costs that do not fluctuate with changes in production level or sales volume. They include salaries, rents, insurance, etc. Despite your best efforts, these are really difficult to change.

G - Gross Income: The total income from all sources before taxes or other deductions. This has nothing to do with money being nasty, even if our mums told us don't play with money because it is dirty.

H - Hedge: Making an investment to reduce the risk of adverse price movements in an asset. You may hedge your bets, i.e. not put all your eggs in one basket... it can be useful in a crisis to have things spread around.

I - Interest Rate: The proportion of a loan that is charged as interest to the borrower, typically expressed as an annual percentage of the loan outstanding. Also known as small print that nobody ever looks at.

J - Joint Venture: A business agreement in which two or more parties agree to pool their resources for the purpose of accomplishing a specific task. This task can be a new project or any other business activity. Often used to leverage online audiences.

K – Kickback: This is an illegal payment in a business or personal setting intended as compensation for preferential treatment. Like tipping a card dealer to get the best hand. It's also used to describe payments acquired via affiliate marketing opportunities which have varying levels of legal requirements for disclosure that are sometimes ignored.

L - Liability: In financial accounting, a liability is defined as the future sacrifices of economic benefits that the entity is obliged to make to other entities. We all tend to have someone in our family or friendship circle that is a bit of a liability.

M - Mortgage: A loan to finance the purchase of property, usually with specified payment periods and interest rates. If you are lucky enough to acquire one, it's that big, scary word that reminds you every month why living in a van down by the river might not be such a bad idea.

N - Net Income: A company's total earnings, calculated by revenue minus the costs of doing business such as depreciation, interest, taxes, and other expenses. Rarely shared when making income claims online.

O - Opportunity Cost: The cost of missing out, of not taking action, of taking too long to take the leap. It can also be about taking one option over another...like choosing between cake or pie; if you choose the cake, your opportunity cost is the delicious pie you didn't get to eat.

P - Portfolio: A range of investments held by a person or organisation. Also a description for a way of working where a person has multiple interests and income streams, i.e. having a portfolio career.

Q - Quick Ratio: An indicator of a company's short-term liquidity. The quick ratio measures a company's ability to meet its short-term obligations with its most liquid assets. On a personal level this is your ability to pay for unplanned car repairs, or expensive vet bills without losing your shit.

R - Return on Investment (ROI): A performance measure used to evaluate the efficiency or profitability of an investment. Some activities, jobs or businesses are loss leading because a full cost recovery approach to assessing the ROI is not taken.

S - Stock: A type of security that signifies ownership in a corporation and represents a claim on part of the corporation's assets and earnings. Can also mean the products you sell that you have available.

T - Turnover: In business accounting, turnover often refers to the total revenue generated by a company in a specific period. It's like a company's "scoreboard" for how well they're doing and is often shared as a way of willy wagging in the online world. In the context of inventory, turnover refers to the number of times an asset is replaced or revolved during a given period. This would be like how often you restock your fridge. For an investment portfolio, turnover refers to the proportion of a portfolio that is bought or sold in a particular period. High turnover implies active trading, like a hyperactive squirrel collecting and stashing away acorns for the winter.

U – Unsecured Loan: A loan that is issued and supported only by the borrowers creditworthiness, rather than by any type of collateral. The lender is basically crossing their fingers and hoping for the best....to some extent the borrower might be too.

V - Value: An assessment of the financial worth of an asset, company, stock, or other investment based on its intrinsic qualities and potential to generate revenue or profit. What something is worth, is not always reflected in what people value it as...or even the price tag attached. In the real world a person's value has nothing to do with this assessment, or at least it shouldn't have.

W - Working Capital: The capital of a business which is used in its day-to-day trading operations. This is the money that keeps the lights on...once it runs out you are in trouble. Closely related to cashflow and something to keep an eye on at all times.

X – Ex's: A sunk cost... I was originally thinking about ex-partners, but can also apply to ex-coaches, ex employees or ex- business partners who turned out to be arseholes. You ain't ever getting that time back... nor the vested interest you had in those people being a valuable part of your life, no matter how brief or expensive the episode... let it go!!!!

Y - Yield: The income return on an investment, such as the interest or dividends received from holding a particular security. It's the reward you get for investing... which can be reinvested indefinitely.

Z - Zero-Sum Game: This is a situation in which one person's gain is equivalent to another's loss, so the net change in wealth or benefit is zero. A pie-eating contest might be a good example - the more pie you eat, the less is left for everyone else.

I hope you found this useful.

Which words would you further add to this list?

### How NOT to be Broke Top Tip

Why not make a list of financial terms you still don't understand, concepts that need to be more front of mind for you to increase your wealth.

Get comfortable with not understanding things, make peace with your ignorance and knowledge gaps, and rather than think that money is something that only the rich can understand make a commitment to increasing your financial literacy and income generating skillset moving forward.

Keep an eye on the language you use...start with never describing yourself as broke, EVER AGAIN.

**Money (n.)** mid-13c., *monie*, "funds, means, anything convertible into money;"

Extended by early 19c. to include paper recognised and accepted for coin.

CHAPTER 1

# *HOPE IS NOT A STRATEGY*

***While hope is essential for optimism and motivation in business, relying on it alone as a solopreneur can lead to inaction and the catastrophic avoidance of your current reality. A robust strategy however will turn your hope into tangible outcomes that can be measured and built upon... and then you can't help but find success and good fortune.***

Work hard. Play nice. And be kind to those less fortunate than you in life.

OH... and *"whatever you do Julie, don't get pregnant".*

Those were pretty much the guidelines I was given growing up.

Simple rules to follow if I wanted to have a successful, respectful and happy life.

Work hard, play nice, be kind.

It all sounded pretty simple.

I could do that.

As a working class girl growing up in the Catholic state school system in East London, it was all about towing the line, learning to be subservient for our future husbands, without losing hope that we could also one day do something worthwhile with our lives besides bearing children.

Born in the summer of 1978, I was a GenX-er born into a time of shifting societal norms, especially for women. I mean shit, we had Madonna AND a female prime minister for goodness sake, surely things would be on the up for a bright ambitious girl like me.

*"What do you want to be when you grow up Julie?"*

I was 12 and about to pick my options for my GCSE's so I guess it was a pretty relevant question. I had been asked this many times before, but this was the first time that someone had asked and genuinely cared about my answer.

*"I don't care Sir... anything... I just don't want to be poor"*

That's when I saw the look, the look that said *"Creffield you are on your last warning"* and quickly changed tact, determined not to end up in detention once again.

*"What about teacher, sir?"* I shouted at the top of my voice which received a giggle from my friends, and a strange exchange of looks between the two members of staff in the small and slightly frowsy room.

Dr Betts, our school's designated careers teacher was a short, round man who always wore a 3-piece suit, and sported a very bad combover, he also taught Latin... because I mean Latin was always going to be useful on the mean streets of East London.

Mrs Betts, his wife was taller, a slight lady, stylish and kind, she taught Home Economics and Modern Languages if I remember right, and was helping her husband that day to manage this particularly unruly class of 12- and 13-year old girls.

*"How about becoming a nursery nurse Julie, you'd be good at that"* she said hopefully as she fiddled around in the boxes looking for the relevant pamphlet *"You already help your mum out with all those kids at home don't you...? You'd be a natural"*

I don't remember there being a box that said "Entrepreneurship" or "Start Your Own Business", neither do I remember any of my peers expressing an interest in self-employment. To be fair we didn't talk much about our futures at all.

*"Yes, great idea"* came the enthusiastic if but a little patronising response from Dr Betts, who was hoping to be able to move swiftly onto the next girl in the line, as there were still a lot to get through.

*"You'd make for a great nursery nurse Julie"*

*"Erm that will be a BIG FAT nope from me sir"* I said boldly.

They were right I did have 5 siblings at home, but I couldn't think of anything worse than having to run around after snotty toddlers all day. And I knew, even back then that nursery nurses were not very well paid, or very well respected.

My Aunt Kim was a nursery nurse, and her husband, my mums older brother Geoff, was a heating engineer and they always seemed grumpy, she spent all his money, and he went fishing at the weekend to get away from the kids... theirs and the others that always seemed to be hanging out at their home.

*"Nah Miss, I think I will stick with teaching, that way I can come back 'ere and we can drink coffees in the staff room together innit?"*

The thing is, I didn't really want to be a teacher. I wanted to be a writer. I wanted to travel. I wanted adventure. I wanted a job on my own terms. I didn't want to be told what to do. I didn't want to wear a uniform... especially not a brown one.

But most of all, quite genuinely, and not for laughs this time, I really didn't want to be poor.

I already understood that being poor meant you had fewer choices. Being poor meant relationships were fraught. Being poor meant people looked down at you. Life was harder for everyone involved. The problem I had though, was I had no idea how not to be poor, as that was all I could see around me. It's all I knew.

All I had... aside from that shocking careers advice, was hope, and those messages of *work hard, play nice and be kind to those less fortunate than me*. Even if my teachers and my parents didn't think I could make something of my life, I had a strong belief I could.

The ancient Greeks pinpointed "hope" as a crucial gift to help with all the evil and suffering of the world, but hope alone is NOT enough in business or in life, and I am on a mission to change what Euripides called "man's curse".

Business studies wouldn't become an option at GCSE level for another 5 years at St Angela's Convent School for Girls... around the same time mandatory typing classes were abolished, so the only reference I had of anyone being an entrepreneur or a millionaire was Rodney and Delboy from *Only Fools and Horses*, and their lives hardly looked glamorous, did they?

And then there was that film in the 80's with Bette Midler...*Working Girl*, she worked in a big office in the city, and they tried to screw her over until she had a make-over and became all bad boss. Oh, and then *Baby Boom*, remember that? Where Diane Keating set up a baby food business after becoming a single mum, and then became super wealthy. So maybe there were references, I just wasn't picking up on them back then.

To be honest I never had any intention of becoming an entrepreneur, but as a child my desire to make money was rife, and my creativity and tenacity to acquire it knew no bounds. I was always on a money-making mission: penny for the guy, delivering taxi cards, a paper round, babysitting, setting up a library in my brothers bedroom and charging for late returns.

My mum often says:

*"You could always make something out of nothing you"* and trust me this was never said as a compliment, not then and not now.

My Mum just doesn't see why I would ever choose to work for myself. All she sees is the risk, the uncertainty, the having to stand out rather than fit in and keep your head down... the way she had been taught was the right way for girls to succeed growing up.

She was always on my case to do something more traditional. She would have loved to see me become a nursery nurse, or a teacher, safe professions that she understood and could happily talk to the neighbours about.

I will never forget going round to my Mum's house a few years after starting my first online business to tell her I had secured a 6-week TV appearance on ITV's *This Morning* show, you know only the biggest daytime TV show in the country, only to be asked,

*"When are you going to get a proper job, Rose will be starting school soon, surely that's the plan"*

By then growing my business was the plan, not being in a position where I was made redundant by another fucker in a bad suit was the plan, showing my daughter that she could be, do and have whatever she wanted in life, regardless of what career path she chooses, that was the plan.

I think she has given up now, we rarely talk about my work, and that feels like a safer space for us both to occupy. Less triggering, less opportunity for her to put her foot in it, and me to get annoyed.

I never set out to be in business, I never chose it, I just kind of fell into it. It chose me.

For sure I had a few high-level full-time jobs when I eventually graduated from Uni, but I already had a wealth of freelance work experience by then, and perhaps I was always destined for entrepreneurship.

You see I have always been able to notice the gaps, the needs, the injustices and I have this in built ability to come up with creative solutions for addressing them. I have always been a bit of a maverick, have never liked being told what to do, and am multi-passionate, so perhaps it was written in the stars.... oh and of course I should probably mention my undiagnosed, but highly probably ADHD traits.

My daughter Rose at aged 6 told me,

*"An entrepreneur is someone who fixes other people's problems and makes loads of money"*

Can't really argue with that.

Did you know in the UK that SME's (Small to medium size enterprises) account for 99.9% of the UK's business population? Small business owners create 61% of all employment, fancy that?

See, those careers teachers didn't know shit back then... there really should have been a box on entrepreneurship on those career room shelves.

However, it turns out there are a lot of people out there right now peddling nonsensical career and business advice that isn't going to get you where you want in life...particularly with the rate of technological change, in this post pandemic world, with all of the uncertainties in the economy that have arisen from those crazy few years.

So, is entrepreneurship REALLY the answer?

For all of us?

Should we all be aspiring to be our own boss, to create multiple passive income streams and then all relocate to Mexico to drink Matcha teas on the beach?

If so we will just need to learn how to do it right? To make all that money. We will need to find the secret sauce, the right strategy, and then we can ALL become millionaires...I mean Rachel Rogers wrote a book telling us we should and we can,

*"I want you to have more money than you've ever had before. Because when you have more money, you have more options in life."*

I am in total agreement with her on that point by the way...but do we ALL have to become millionaires in order to get there? Is having extraordinary amounts of money the only way to have true freedom?

I'm not so sure.

Do we ALL have to be millionaires, or 6 figure business owners, to be considered proper?

I'm also not sure how useful that is as a motivating message for small business owners anyway. In fact I'd go as far to say that for MOST as it stands, it can actually be counterproductive.

Because here's the thing... Fewer than 8000 businesses in the UK are considered large. Out of the 5.58 million SMEs currently active in the UK, more than 4 million of those have zero employees... so are in fact microbusinesses or sole traders.

So how many solopreneur businesses are there that are actually turning over 7 figures? How many of them are able to take out of the business anything close to 7 figures in dividends or salary? How many of them are doing this without a team, or enormous audiences acquired from a previous life or pre-existing celebrity...that's before we talk about those that simply have access to unlimited supplies of money and other peoples expertise to enable that growth?

Welcome my friend to the crazy world of Solopreneurship, where all is not what it seems.

Where it is so easy to get sucked into the idea of becoming a millionaire, whether that's your original goal or not... you know, cos why not?

After all, as the national lottery slogan says,

*"It could be you!!!"*

So what indeed is a solopreneur...and are you even one of the gang?

**Solopreneur... A person who sets up and runs a business on their own.**

Also known as, the person responsible for pretty much EVERYTHING that goes on in their business, heading up Strategy, Sales, Product Design AND Delivery, Customer Service, Finance, Tech, Marketing, PR...oh and HR...not of course in relation to staff (remember we don't have any) but responsible for ensuring our own health and safety, wellbeing and professional development, as the sole employee in the job that we have so kindly created for ourselves.

Sound familiar?

Oh, hang on, you have a VA? And some business buddies? And let's not forget the hundreds of people you have connected with on Facebook groups so you feel less alone? But how come then most days we are still filled with fear, dread and overwhelm? Just me?

Because we are human beings with emotions, and we care deeply about our work. We also have the added pressure of having our nervous system activated emotionally day in and day out as we navigate the online world having us all in a bit of a whirl.

When I say hope is not a strategy...this doesn't check on your hope levels...but alone, you may find you bouncing from hopefulness to hopelessness like a bleeding yoyo...and we can't be having that.

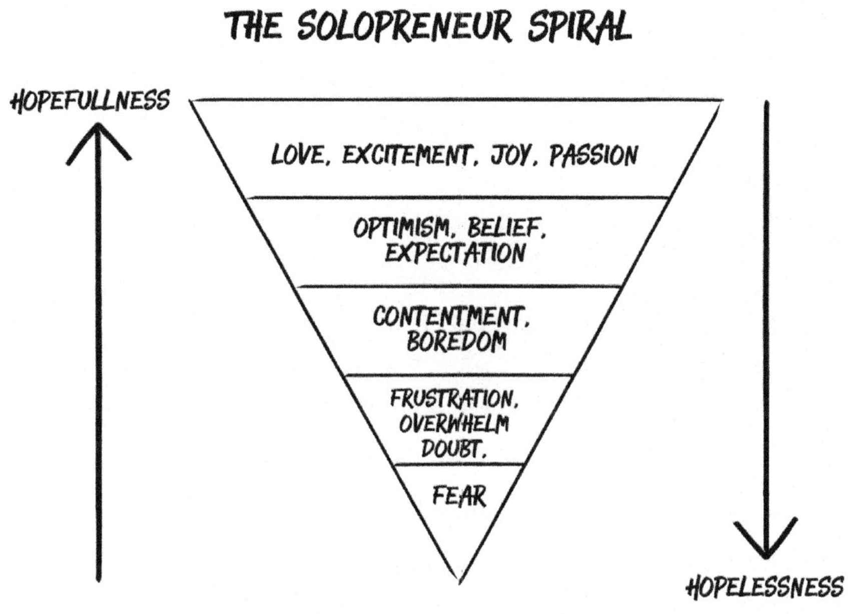


Ultimately the buck stops with you, doesn't it?

When all is said and done you are the one who has to make the business viable, you are the one who cares most about your venture, who is putting in all the time, effort and possibly even money from your savings or earned revenue... It's your business and you must carry the load... quite literally, right?

It's a lot... the question though, is it worth it?

Small businesses account for half of the UK's turnover... a whopping £2.3 trillion... which I guess leaves us with the question of who exactly is making all that money? And why do you still feel broke every month?

Now, I am not saying that making a good living from your business is not possible, nor that having a multi six or seven figure business isn't something we could be working towards if we want... I just want to offer some perspective.

I want you to move forward with your eyes open, so that you can make informed decisions about your next steps, because whether you like it or not there is a legacy, an impact, ongoing repercussions to you choosing this path.

I just don't want you relying purely on hope and a prayer... or god forbid the laws of attraction... not by themselves anyway.

As a business legacy strategist, I have worked with thousands of SME's and many larger companies and organisations that support entrepreneurs, and I can tell you it is truly shocking what I have seen when we start talking numbers.

- How many hours are being spent in and on the business
- How much money has been invested or reinvested
- What traction folks are getting (or not getting)
- What sacrifices are being made in the hope that there will be a brighter future... at some point
- What business owners are REALLY left with at the end of each financial year, and more importantly at the end of their lives

This is not just a problem I see with my own clients. I have invested in tons of business growth programmes and worked with some of the most well-known coaches around the world... and it is a similar story wherever I go.

It's a pandemic in its own right.... perhaps even amplified by the actual "Pandemic" when everyone and their dog was forced to engage in the online world unlike any other time in history. I mean if you were not engaging in laughing yoga, or sourdough for beginners courses delivered via zoom, where even were you?

It's not been our business content going viral, for most of us it's all that unrequited hope and expectation around building a 6-, 7-, 8-figure business regardless of your capabilities that has become like a virus, folks have truly caught the entrepreneurship bug... and as far as I can tell there is no vaccine on the horizon to come save us.

There are literally millions and millions of solopreneurs hustling their way through life, living in hope, avoiding or not understanding the real strategy required to create a sustainable business... and rarely looking at the numbers that matter.

There is an incredible cost to all of this, the living in the future rather than the living in the now, putting off or compromising other things, which further contributes to us feeling broke in one way or another.

Because let's not forget, being broke isn't just about not having any money. It is often a combination of factors that exacerbate each other, leading to neglect, decay and eventually complete collapse... if you let it get that far.

I don't want you to feel broke, get broke, be seen as broke in any aspect of your life... especially not your business life, it is too important. The world needs healthy, enthusiastic, well rounded small business owners... for a start the worlds economy would literally crash without us.

Think of Solopreneur safety and security like a 4 legged chair...having legs of equal length makes a chair totally stable, if one or more of the legs is shorter than the other we then have a wobbly chair. It may still stand... but lose one leg all together and then it will fall over and you might fall off it and hurt yourself.

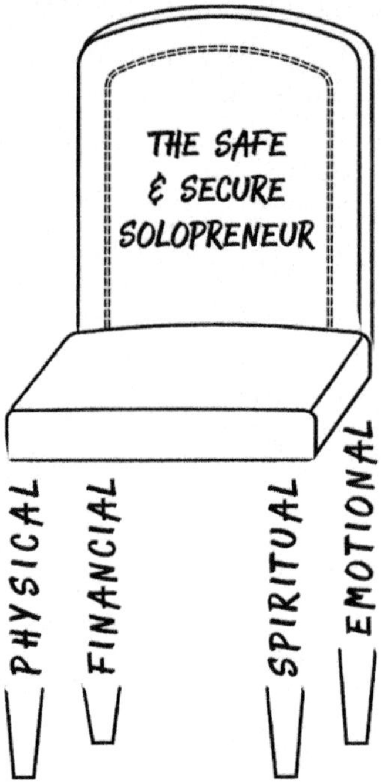


You can survive on 3 legs...yes, we are now talking about a stool (like a bar stool, not a poo stool let's not get the two confused), the load still has to be evenly spread (ok who's still thinking about poo?)...

4 legs gives you the greatest level of safety and security, which is why we don't generally put our elders or our little kids on high stools right? So let's look at the 4 areas...the 4 legs that may feel a bit wobbly for you right now.

The 4 areas where you could be feeling broke.

1. Financially Broke... where a person is without the necessary resources to fund their life, this could be in terms of basic needs like food and shelter, or other desires such as luxury items, experiences or travel

2. Emotionally Broke... where a person is depleted of their emotional resources due to perhaps chronic stress, a lack of self-care, unhealthy relationships, a lack of emotional support.
3. Spiritually Broke... where someone feels a lack of purpose, meaning, or connection in life. This is caused by ignoring our Inner Values or living contrary to one's deeply held beliefs which can lead to a sense of spiritual emptiness.
4. Physically Broke... where the body is not functioning at its best due to neglect or damage. Not exercising, poor nutrition, a lack of sleep, substance abuse, ignoring health niggles.

And, of course, the environment can create a further challenge, meaning that the chair can become wobbly even if you have all the above sorted. The wobblier the chair to start with though, the less likely you can ride out environmental factors.

So how broke do you really feel right now?

There have been many times in my life where I have felt less than. Where I have allowed other people to determine my wealth, or where I have compared myself to metrics of success that left me feeling like I wasn't good enough, or like that kind of success would never be possible for me.

I have felt broke.

There have also been times where I have actively sabotaged my own success, especially in my late twenties and early thirties, where I burned the candle at both ends, spent frivolously, chose terrible boyfriends, and didn't take care of my body.

I didn't value myself much at all... despite appearing confident to the rest of the world. I though all of us young women out there trying to make their way in life were doing the same, trying to prove we could have it all.

It would get to the point where it was clear I was spiralling, where I was losing control, where I had gone too far. Something shocking would happen, be that financially, or with a relationship breakdown, or a bout of unexplained fatigue and depression, and deep down I would know something needed to change.

At times I took fearless action, applied for a new job, or designed a new freelance offering. But sometimes I would just sit and let my life spiral hoping and praying that something would come along to change everything.

*"You never know, I might win the lottery"* I'd joke, when my credit cards were all maxed out again, and I felt the need for some kind of adventure.

Did you know the odds of becoming a millionaire as a solopreneur are much like those of winning the lottery... and yet we are still led to believe as small business owners that it is possible, that reaching the 7 figure turnover point is the way forward for all of us... almost like we are duty bound to be looking for that size of business, otherwise there must be something wrong with us.

Millions of people around the world play lotteries as they feel like they have no other hope of ever seeing money like that, when in fact with most odds of winning they should expect to hit the jackpot once every 250,000 years.

But the cost of playing is negligible right? And so, hope wins. We keep giving it a go. We remain broke, or at least that's the undercurrent, the underlying feeling that keeps us stuck, keeps us in the system.

The truth is that the cost of staying on "The Broke" train is too great, the risk of never reaching your potential, and always living for some distant time in the future too damaging to your physical and mental health and your sense of self-worth.

And that's before we look at the knock-on effect of your situation on your loved ones, and future generations who are looking to you for guidance and inspiration.

It is time for action... NOT hope.

Don't get me wrong there is a place for hope, but it must sit alongside a robust strategy and inspired, aligned, consistent action, especially when it comes to making money and changing the world with your business venture.

And so let me introduce to you our first **How Not to Be Broke Principle**...of which there are 12 in this book., which, of course, in numerology and many other schools of thought represents the full circle of life.

1. Hope is NOT a strategy

I am not against you using hope to drive you forward, what I am against however is hope being the main driver. As emotional human beings you can see why we do this, that sense of better times ahead is sometimes the only thing that gets us up in the morning.

It's how we all got through COVID after all isn't it?

But what then if we lose hope (and there will be points where we do), when business just becomes too difficult, or something in life causes hardship or heartache and we literally can't face the enormity of what we are trying to do... what are we left with?

The cost of using hope as our primary motivation is too great, it leaves us too vulnerable, it may even blinker us to the reality of what is actually going on in the world, or have us second guess our own ability to transform our lives.

Hoping to have more success in life
Hoping to have more money in your account

Hoping to have better relationships
Hoping that the world gets fairer
Hoping that the cost of your heating bill will go down
Hoping that things will change

Rather than taking sustained action towards those things actually happening, rather than changing your own behaviours and habits... with a sprinkle of hope and optimism to keep us motivated of course.

Being broke is not just about having limited access to resources, it is also a mindset, a feeling that you can't shake off... a sense of hopelessness? YES, but also a feeling of disempowerment, like nothing will ever change even if you do put in the work... because the systems and structures are built that way, and people like you and me don't tend to get a break in this world.

The problem is, there are always examples to the contrary... and that does give us hope. It is why so many of us doom scroll on Instagram, looking for those flickers of *"that could be me"* and *"maybe I could have all of that too, if I work hard enough"*

I have led the most extraordinary life considering my starting point, I have travelled the world, climbed mountains and run marathons; I have met royalty and rubbed shoulders with countless famous people; I've worked with major global brands, and tried all sorts of crazy activities to fuel my ADHD brain and my quest for adventure.

And someone like me shouldn't have been able to.

I have invested heavily in my education and put myself in the right places, chasing that illusive dream of becoming a millionaire. I have had consistent £10K months, I have had 6 figure launches, I have built multiple six figure businesses.

It's been a vibe.

But despite that abundance I have often still felt quite broke.

I have worked my butt off, trying to find success and financial security.

There have been times where I felt there must be something wrong with me. I have been the epitome of feast and famine, and I have had to bounce back from various financial challenges and knocks to my confidence and self-esteem over the years... often caused by the very industry that I am part of.

So, trust me I have seen first-hand how useless hope is as a strategy. No amount of hope would find me new clients, no amount of hope would stop the bills from coming, no amount of hope would magically make things better... action, action and more action is what transformed my life, action and a clear sense of what I actually wanted.

Action ALWAYS led to making more money, hope rarely did. Too much hope often led to me losing money, losing my confidence, losing my sense of self... giving away my power. Hope is just too unreliable as a driver... like a useless boyfriend, the one who keeps promising to do better but never really does.

It isn't just about acquiring unlimited money though.

I realised during the most profitable year of my life, that money wasn't enough of a motivator for me at all, and the pursuit of it was making me ill... it was causing me to fall apart quite literally at the seams... because I wasn't keeping a close enough eye on those other 3 legs.

It didn't matter how much money my Solopreneur business made me, it never fulfilled me, not completely. I always felt like there was another hoop to jump through, another accolade to get before I would feel worthy... something else I was neglecting.

Which is why I have written this book... to create change.

For me, for my clients, and for the army of entrepreneurs out there hoping they can make it, hoping that business success will give them validity, will go some way in plugging those worthiness gaps.

Poverty is subjective, as is the concept of being wealthy and whole... and when we think of those two places (rich and poor) as binary positions this encourages division, it encourages attitudes and behaviours of them and us... weird power games, when really wealth and abundance (like most things) are on a spectrum.

My personal quest to NOT BE BROKE, to ensure my daughter never feels broke like I did growing up is not about making a million pound. Instead, it is to change the patterns in my family (of women in particular) not feeling good enough... and to shine a light for other Solopreneurs who have experienced similar feelings.

Because the truth is, we are NOT broke, but many of the systems and structures that affect our abundance and wellbeing certainly are. Never has there been a time in history (in my humble opinion) where an army of switched on changemakers, business owners with money to spend has been more needed to step in and make the changes that need making on this planet... than NOW.

This book is a call to adventure, but also a practical guidebook to get you taking action. It is an opportunity for you to explore your own position on wealth and to challenge your mindset around what it takes to change your financial situation.

This book is an invitation for you to draw a line in the sand, and to open yourself up to a whole new way of thinking about, and acting on, becoming wealthier. And the key there is the action bit.

This book is mostly a tool to encourage the application of your learning. For you to decide on how you want to use your money and the other resources you have available to you for creating wealth, safety, stability and maybe even systemic change.

This is not about being rich, neither is it just about "Not being poor" but it is about autonomy and having freedom of choice to decide on where you want to be, what you want to have, and how you can share this approach with future generations.

I want you to NEVER feel broke because of the money you have or the money you don't, and I want you to be able to utilise all the other resources available to you to live a life full of meaning and freedom, regardless of what your bank balance says.

Wealth in the wrong hands creates so much hardship for so many others, imagine if the tables were turned, imagine what could happen if more of the world's resources got into the hands of people who really cared about changing this planet for the better?

Shall we get started...time is of the essence?

**How Not to be Broke Top Tip**

Think about what prompted you to buy this book? Listen to the assumptions you are making about how it might be able to support your money journey.

Ask yourself the following questions?

1. Am I REALLY broke?
2. Which areas of my life feel a bit, or a lot, broke?
3. Am I using hope as a strategy in my business and life? If so, where?
4. Am I taking radical self-responsibility for my situation?
5. What is this all costing me?
6. What would I do with my money if I came into a lot of it?

**Freedom (n.)**

Old English *freodom* "power of self-determination, state of free will; emancipation from slavery, deliverance;" see free (adj.) + -dom. Meaning "exemption from arbitrary or despotic control, civil liberty" is from late 14c. Meaning "possession of particular privileges" is from 1570s.

CHAPTER 2

# *RADICAL RESPONSIBILITY...AND WHY WE ALL NEED THIS BOOK*

***Nobody is coming to save you. It's time to take charge of your own financial destiny, because waiting for external rescue, and expecting others to support your success, often leads to disappointment, resentment, or worse still inertia. Know that improving your situation is 100% your responsibility AND totally within your capacity and capability.***

I just want you to take a moment to think about how many books you have already read on the topic of money? How much time have you spent trying to further understand how to increase your business income?

How's that working out for you?

Think about the return on investment you have received so far from your ongoing education (or lack of) in this area and if this is sustainable moving forward. What needs to change? What do you need to lean into? And are you willing to keep using hope as a strategy when it comes to business, instead of rolling up your sleeves and becoming the CEO of your small but perfectly formed venture?

This book is based on 12 foundational principles for creating, managing and leveraging wealth as a solopreneur, my **How NOT to be Broke Manifesto** which you can find in its entirety towards the end of the book

These principles and concepts combined will encourage you to look at your past, your present and your future without shame or shade, and act as a reminder to keep checking in on your money stuff long after you put down this book.

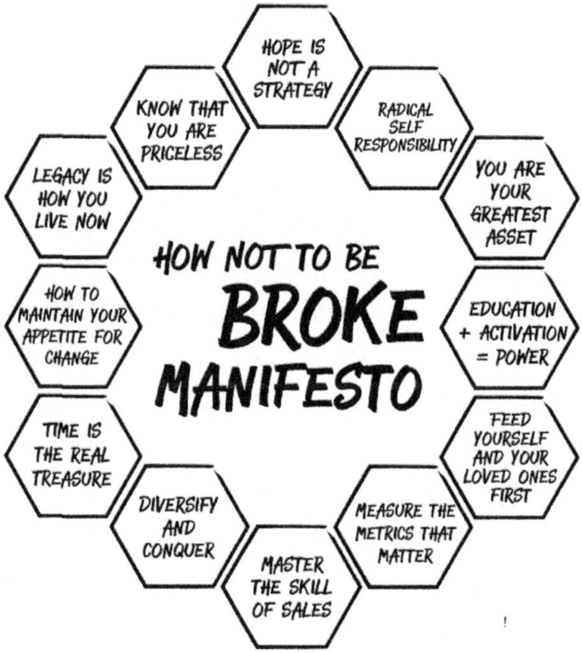


The magic will happen though, when you implement the learning and make changes in your own life and business. Instead of expecting this book to work magic without any of your actual involvement.

So, this is on you... totally on you.

I am not here to save you, and sadly there is nothing you will learn in this book that will make you an overnight millionaire simply by osmosis or having the book half read on a shelf... I have a bookshelf full of business and money books.

No. If you are serious about changing your financial situation, then I want you to use this book as it was designed to be used... as a living breathing experiment on wealth creation, and for that to be successful you need to take fearless action.

We tend to buy self-help and business books because we want something to change. We want to understand how to do (or stop doing) something, and we read them because we feel like perhaps there is some missing trick, some secret sauce that everyone else seems to have but it has alluded you somehow.

Do you know Google once tried to digitize the worlds books and estimated that there were more than 129 million unique books. YES we have reached the tipping point where there are more creators of content than there are consumers.

The truth is there are still not enough books about money written by women.

There are still not enough females accessing venture capital funds or getting angel investment.

There are still not enough examples of women doing well for themselves.

Not by far.

And there are not enough business owners more generally, talking about the messy middle of being in business... you know that bit after the exciting launch and initial growth spurt, but before the euphoria of total world domination.

Plus, last time I checked there wasn't a single book on wealth creation written by a 45 year old plus size single mum from East London...

and who knows, maybe it will be my perspective and my practical application of wealth creation that unlocks the thing that has been sitting dormant in you.

If that happens, then my job here is done.

When I first started my wealth education journey more than a decade ago it was hard to find books on money that were not written by wealthy, white, American men. Things are better than they have been, but it is still mainly cis white males' views on wealth creation that are referred to... as well as them having the monopoly on land ownership, investor boards and so on and so forth.

A popular book on wealth creation I read recently, which was otherwise quite sound, had more than 50 examples of wealthy and successful people, and yet he only referred to 3 women (and yes, you can probably name them).

But even the books that are written about money by women, still tend to be written by women who have already made their millions ... they are the outliers, the 1% and generally speaking, are attractive women with flowing hair and great teeth... and they normally have some level of privilege, even if they won't admit to it fully.

Those books are sometimes nothing more than the top end of a funnel to get you into their high-ticket coaching programmes and are often regurgitated law of attraction style guides for thinking things into existence, with a few personal stories thrown in for good measure.

#sorrynotsorry

This does not make them bad people, nor their books not a great place to start your journey, but I am more interested in the bigger picture, not just the 1% of entrepreneurs that "make it" but the rest of us that are serious about using our businesses as a vehicle for change, even when we can't pump half a million pound into Facebook ads, to reach multiple 7 figure status.

This is my story, but it is also our story. An opportunity for us to look at how we got here, what we need to do to move forward. And it's a rallying cry for change... real systematic and cultural change... that must start with us, on an individual level... we can't wait for the powers that be to make things easy for us, that will never happen.

Radical self-responsibility isn't for the faint hearted. It takes us not from zero to hero, or even victim to hero; no, it takes us from where we are now into the energy of the crusader, the campaigner, the champion of change, knowing it will be hard, knowing the journey won't be smooth, but knowing that the fight will be worth it.

We need a shift in our individual and collective understanding of what it means to be wealthy on our own terms, using our own metrics of success as yard sticks... beyond how much money we have in the bank, or what brand of handbag we carry.

I have been wanting to write *How NOT to be Broke* for several years, but always held myself back because of the fear of judgement. What would people think, what would my family think as I share the early years of my life, what would the people who have seen me struggle financially over the years think?

Who am I to talk about NOT being broke, when I have been with limited funds so often throughout my life... and am nowhere close to being a millionaire (spoiler alert)... oh and I do not own a pair of red bottomed shoes... just so you are clear.

Would being so transparent about the ups and downs of my career, personal finances, and business failures make me less credible as a life and business strategist? Or more so?

But that is the power of words: the written word, the spoken word, the words of advice shared amongst family members and friends, the ones used to create new narratives, new understandings and much needed new perspectives of the world.

I do not need to be a guru; I simply need to have a voice... as do you.

A voice that sounds different to all the others out there, one that lands differently, that has a different perspective. One that stands fully grounded in its truth.

If we only ever read books from people who are extremely wealthy, or financial gurus who speak in jargon, where do we access different, but still useful, narratives that create connection and a better more visceral understanding of money and how to make more of it available to us?

*How Not to Be Broke* isn't just about diagnosing the problem; it's about offering real, tangible solutions; it's about helping you understand and navigate this financial maze with confidence; breaking down the complex financial concepts into relatable, understandable advice, so you can take the right action.

Despite being written off at school, and failing my GCSE maths twice, here I am, a woman in my forties with 2 degrees behind me, author of over a dozen books, living in a million pound barn conversion in the countryside... with the ability to ramp up my income as and when it suits.

You will find no romanticism here about my path to financial stability, dealing with 5 redundancies, becoming a single parent, ending up in hospital with COVID, my mental health having far too many low points to mention in one book.

What you will hear is the truth, my truth, what I see day in and day out with the incredible business owners I meet, some of whom still struggle, not because they are not amazing at what they do, but they don't have the privilege that so many of the super successful people have... or they have conflicting barriers and challenges that they are navigating, many of which come back to the inequality that exists in our financial structures and systems.

And so, my only request of you the reader:

Please don't read this book and believe that anything significant will change just by reading it. If you are serious about changing your financial story, and possibly even the trajectory of your life and the lives of your loved ones, then please...

TAKE ACTION.

I have left lots of white space for you to make notes... what comes up for you? How does this apply to your situation. Keep a running list of actions, things to try, things to share with your business buddies or loved ones.

Test my theories, challenge them, challenge your own. Go out there and make your money work better for you, find additional resources, leverage the assets you have. Make today your Day 1.

To help you further, I have collated some FREE resources for you, and I also run a fun sales challenge 3 times a year to take the practical application of this book into your life and business. You can find this all at:

www.juliecreffield.com/broke

Oh, and did I mention we are going to attempt to change our financial situation in 12 months? Yep, that's right. When my life fell apart catastrophically in January 2023, just 6 months before deciding to write this book, I gave myself a year... turned out I only needed 6 months to get me back to baseline, and the next 6 are about testing these methods further so that I never feel broke again.

That's my WHY for writing this book.

When I realised I was a month away from becoming homeless (again) after 25 years of hard graft, I knew something significant needed to change, and that something significant was me.

So, just to be clear...before we proceed.

The opposite of broke is not fixed, neither is it rich... the Ying to the Yang of broke is to be secure, and this book will explore my *How NOT to be Broke Model* for safety and security as a small business owner

S - See (Your vision for financial safety and security)
E - Embrace (The journey... the highs and the lows)
C - Commit (The long term investment and required change)
U - Utilize (Your existing knowledge, resources and assets)
R - Remember (Your inherent value and always address your basic needs first)
E - Evaluate (Your financial progress frequently)

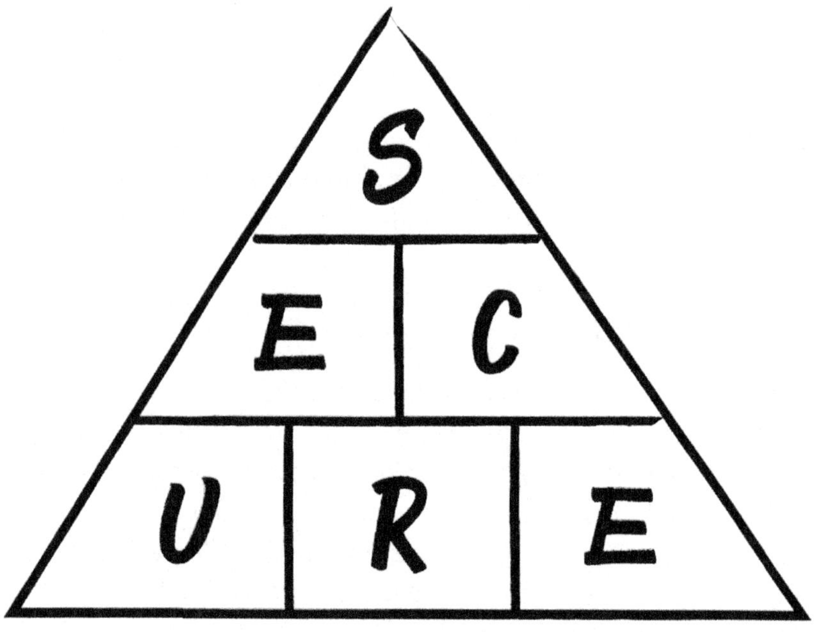


The Egyptians were onto something when they started building Pyramids...built to last, come rain or shine. With strong foundations in place anything is possible. Start at which ever corner feels most relevant for you, work on one mindset shift at a time if you must, but know when all six of these are in place you are laughing as a Solopreneur...can't nobody knock you down.

This book is my commitment to change. This book is my line in the sand. This book is my public declaration that I am NOT broke... and I never was. Instead I am moving forward, embracing the highs and lows that come with being in business, but from a place of self-enforced safety and security.

Remember we are on this journey together, and I am rooting for you, just like I am rooting for me.

### How Not to be Broke Top Tip

Allocate a specific paper journal or notebook just for wealth creation or check out my accompanying How Not to be Broke planner, which includes all the Top Tip Exercises, plus additional tools and resources.

And keep your journal somewhere special, honour it, give it the treatment it deserves... as this may well turn out to be an important document, an artefact for future learning in years to come... just like some of my journals and diaries have.

Commit to checking in with your money stuff at least weekly... even if only for 10-15 minutes.... trust me this tip alone is probably the hardest AND the most powerful one you can commit to.

See how your understanding of and beliefs about money change throughout this book. Try out the suggested exercises. Do the Audit. Make the budgets. Work out the real cost of not acting. Create lists. Store your ideas. Do the important forgiveness work.

Information and knowledge are not enough these days to move you up the ladder, it is the application of what we learn through taking inspired, fearless action where we see the real results.

**Wealth (n.)** Mid -13c., "happiness," also "prosperity in abundance of possessions or riches," from Middle English *wele* "well-being"

## CHAPTER 3

# *YOU ARE YOUR GREATEST ASSET*

***Investing our excess income is a sensible route to wealth, but if investing in big business, stocks and shares feel like too much of a stretch, investing in yourself can yield the greatest return of all... even with small contributions, because much like a traditional investment portfolio there is a compound effect, and we are here for the long game.***

What this means in practice is prioritizing your personal and professional development, looking after your mental and physical health, and staying firmly on that path of continuous learning when it comes to money and all things success.

It means knowing, valuing and protecting your true worth.

You have unlimited resources at your disposal as a small business owner, even if you don't realise it yet. What you lack in money in the bank, can totally be offset with your creativity or your drive... at least to some extent.

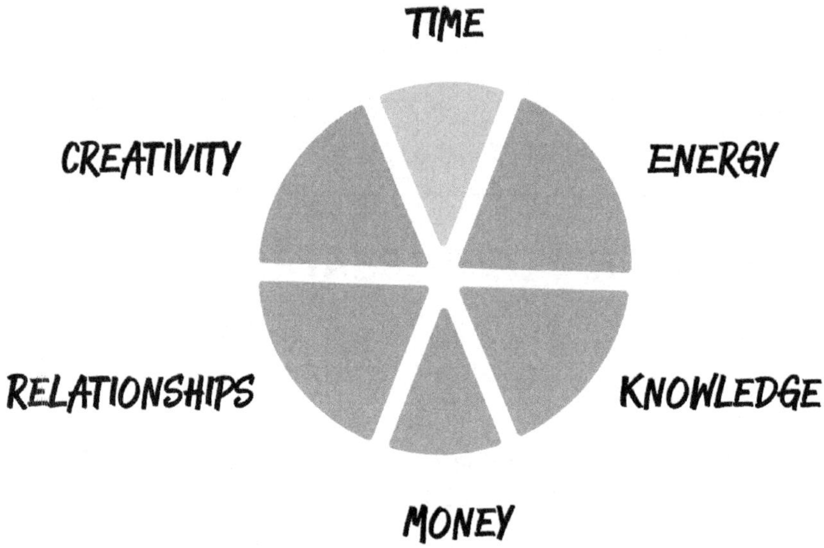


The key to leveraging all of the resources above however is you...and it comes down to you thinking you are worthy of success.

I remember my nan always used to press a silver coin into the hand of each new-born baby that come into our large East London family, it was a tradition. That would literally have been my first interaction with money... and it always felt like some kind of shady practice, done on the sly not to mention potentially dangerous in terms of money being "dirty" and carrying germs.

One of my early memories of money as a kid was crawling on my hands and knees in my parents' bedroom, while my siblings tried not to laugh, so I could reach into my dad's jean pockets to grab whatever money was there... I knew that taking the paper money would get me in trouble, but he was unlikely to miss the coins, so they were fair game.

My mum however was always counting coins, trying to find them down the back of the sofa, and rummaging in coat pockets... we always needed money for various things we were doing at school, or to pay the milkman, or the man who collected the money for the Pools.

When I was older and my parents had divorced, I would walk to dad's place of work to collect my pocket money, a trick he'd use to get us to visit him, not to teach us anything particularly about managing our money... he didn't always give us that £1 coin... sometimes we'd have to settle for a can of fizzy drink or a chocolate bar, and other times we would leave with nothing.

So, as you can see, my early memories of money are all over the place.

Rituals, blessings, stealing, shame, gambling, uncertainty, bribery... and all before I'd even reached my teens. Is it any wonder my own money mindset has contributed to such financial highs and lows over the years?

Growing up, we were acutely aware of the lack of resources in our household, there never seemed to be enough money, enough time, enough attention, enough seats to sit on when people visited, and maybe even enough love.

This wasn't always the case, but I felt the shift when we moved from our small two up two down terraced house in East Ham, to our 5 bedroom semi-detached home with its through lounge and attic room in Upton Park.

The house was big, but it was sparce, we were living beyond our means and the tension between my parents was palpable.

My dad was a gambler, and a drinker... but also a wanna-be entrepreneur by all accounts, a wheeler-dealer of sorts. He worked as a cashier in a petrol garage, but somehow owned a greyhound at one point, and would come home ladened with gifts, stuff he'd got off the back of a lorry or bought off one of his many associates.... I assume he had his fingers in many pies.

Shell suits, women's dresses, cases of fizzy drinks, bottles of scotch.... one time he arrived home in a Porsche, a car he had won in a card game, but had to give back a few days later under duress. Dad lived in the moment, but also dreamed about having more... however, he didn't always face up to the responsibility of being a dad.

By this point Mum was in her early 30s, with 6 kids under the age of 10, and only a couple of years clear of having what was initially considered as terminal cancer. With just one income coming in, 6 kids, and a massive mortgage, I just can't see how they managed financially... even if things were cheaper in the 80s.

It was typical feast and famine in our household, we had holidays some years, I had a new BMX bike aged 10, and we had day trips to Southend, where we were given a couple of quid to fuck off for a few hours so my Dad could chat to his friends in the pub... oh and they somehow always had money for fags.

But there were also times where there was no food in the cupboard, where we couldn't do the things our friends did at the weekend, and I remember a year where there was no money for new school shoes in September, and I went back in a pair of summer sandals.

I never really knew why it was like this, as nobody ever talked to us explicitly about money when we were kids. This felt unsettling, I never quite knew where I was at. What I was allowed to ask for in life, what was too much, what wasn't enough?

In my first year of secondary school my parents finally divorced, and the following year our big old house would be repossessed, seeing Mum start her journey as a single mum of 6 kids living in temporary accommodation miles away from her support network, and our 3 different schools.

I will never forget the last night in our big house in Central Park Road.

Bailiffs had come to take the remaining valuables from our home including our TV which felt incredibly cruel considering the makeup of our household. The rest of our personal belongings had been packed up and put into my grandad's lock up while the council attempted to rehouse us.

Mum made it an adventure. The electricity had been cut off, most of the furniture and our belongings were gone, but we had chips from the chip shop to share, with two big bottles of fizzy pop, sat in the front room with a car headlight hooked up to a battery that my Grandad had sorted out for us...wondering about what our new house would be like.

The next day we moved 9 miles away to Walthamstow....home of pop band E17, and Europe's longest street market. We lived in a cul-de-sac on the edge of a housing estate, where the kids played out way past the street lights going on, and we had more freedom than we had ever had before.

It was that freedom that saw me starting my first business, a partnership with my older brother Gary which saw us knocking door to door and asking "Would you like us to wash your car?".

My brother who was 14 at the time had invested £5 of his birthday money towards buying the important materials we needed, "We defo need a chamise leather if anyone is going to take us seriously" he told me.

We washed two cars that day at £5 a pop, he made his initial investment back, and we spent the rest on saveloy and chips on the way home, slightly deflated that car washing wasn't going to make us rich any time soon.

I have super fond memories of the year I spent in that temporary home. I didn't feel broke, even though I know my Mum was on her knees, as she navigated the benefits system, and waited for her divorce settlement to come through.

A teacher at school once said to me: *"Julie, you will end up just like your mum, loads of kids and on benefits"*

That stuck with me for many years. The shame that teacher tried to inflict on me and my mum. The embarrassment she caused in the moment in front of my friends. The lack of empathy. The judgements. The assumptions. The complete lack of compassion.

Poverty isn't always the thing which keeps us stuck, the shame of it however can be super debilitating, literally stopping us from taking action to change our situations. The risk of shame, is enough to keep us playing safe, to keep us from asking for help, to keep us from asking the right questions, from maintaining our boundaries, from maintaining our self-worth.

*"Have you no shame?"*
*"You should be ashamed of yourself"*
*"Shame on you"*

See how it is weaponised?

The comment from that teacher that day made me believe that this is what everyone felt about folks who needed government assistance, people who had free school meals, people who were poor. My mum did claim income support when my Dad left her, and probably for a few years before that, as she had 6 kids under the age of 10 and was battling Hodgkin's Lymphoma... so I am pretty sure my Dad's cashier job couldn't have carried us all even if he had wanted it to.

My mum had paid into the tax system, she had been a legal secretary straight out of school, and worked up until she had her 3rd child. When we were all teenagers my Mum went back out to work which must have been super challenging after all she had been through, and she spent over a decade working in the voluntary sector and the education system in Tower Hamlets.

She raised 6 hard working human beings who have all gone on to raise their own children, or foster in some cases. We were never encouraged to get council houses, or to sign on, it was instilled in us from an early age that we were to get jobs and to become self-sufficient... maybe that is due to the stigma that very much still exists around people in receipt of state benefits.

When I had to briefly turn to Job Seekers Allowance in 2013 after being made redundant while pregnant, the shame was unbearable. I couldn't find a job that would cover my childcare, and I only managed to tolerate the god-awful way the staff talk to you in that place for a few months, before choosing to go back into entrepreneurship again.

When cashflow issues relating to my most recent redundancy saw me call up the local council to talk through an unpaid Council Tax bill, I burst into tears, not because of the shame, but because this time the lady on the end of the phone was just so kind and compassionate as she outlined all of the benefits I was eligible for,

*"Make the applications love, it's what these benefits are designed for. You have paid enough into the system over the years, and you will find work again"*

I didn't end up making the applications in the end, as something shifted in me that day along with those tears. It was a reminder of the past traumas though, which still live within me. The disempowerment of needing to let others carry me.

Maybe there was also some residual shame, maybe going down the benefit route would have caused me to second guess my own ability to come to my own rescue in the long term, so maybe it was for the best, but no judgement, we all have to do what we all have to do.

What I have learned to realise is that most people (rich, poor or somewhere in the messy middle) have some lived experience of a time where they felt like they didn't have enough resources to do what they wanted or needed to do, to cover bills, to pay for the essentials, to make the life and business choices they want to. Most people have experienced a time where they have perhaps had to compromise on their desires, their values, maybe even their ethics.

For some, not having enough is temporary, for others this is a more permanent experience, but with both comes a layer of shame and frustration which makes the whole situation more painful than it needs to be, often extending the hardship further.

Asking for help for many groups, single mums, people of colour, those from certain religious backgrounds, it literally feels unthinkable, and when translated into a business setting the same rules apply, leading to undercharging, over delivering, not being able to trust people enough to participate in collaborations and partnerships.

Now my story of growing up in adverse poverty most definitely won't be your story, and let's face it there is very little you can do as a child to change your financial situation or the circumstances you are born into. But my story, just like yours, can be a driver for financial success, especially when you give yourself time and space to explore it and tackle the money mindset blocks that get in the way of success.

We have generational bonds, ancestorial ties to poverty, some of which are incredibly hard to shake off... I know I feel incredibly connected to the stories of struggle, and hardship from the various lines of my family tree... and combined with my own lived experience of feast and famine, my money story is complex.

As a solopreneur your money story will be impacting almost every transaction that happens in your business. The way you price, the way you spend your time, the scale of your ambition, the boundaries you have (or don't have), your ability to take rejection or to be visible online, and how you deal with conflict.

I mean take your pricing as an example, how many times have you been told to *"Charge Your Worth, Charge Your Worth!!!"* how on earth are you supposed to quantify that? What do we base that on? And what do we make it mean when people don't want to pay our rates?

Can you see, through some of the stories I have already shared about my early years, how my sense of self-worth is fragile, and that's before I head down the path of sharing my dating track record, my life long struggle with body image and the stigma that comes with being a single mum lol...but it's all connected.

Remember I told you my mum would often say:

*"You could always make something out of nothing, you"*

That hurts.

Looking at that phrase now, it hurts. I wish I had pulled her up on it earlier and told her, *"I am the something Mum" "I am an amazing, resourceful, resilient human being, who put herself through university, and has made her own way in life with very little help from anyone else...that's not nothing"*

I am sure it was not her intention for me to interpret those words in a way that implies I am simply winging this whole business success thing, but remember words matter... and in my working class family, "banter" and "taking the piss" out of each other is par for the course.

Regardless of our upbringing, the life we were born into, or even our sense of self-worth, we will have picked up beliefs, behaviours and a mindset around money and success informed by our parents and the other adults around us... and in turn their beliefs, behaviours and mindset would have been informed by their parents...sprinkled with a bit of lived experience and the impact of the specific cultural and economic environment they live in.

And so the cycle continues.

Educating ourselves and strengthening our money mindset is only one part of the solution, because even when we commit to empowering ourselves and changing our circumstances as a business owner, there are some common pitfalls that can lead to financial instability at any time in our life for EVERYONE, regardless of their employment status, of social standing.

As Selina Todd explains in her book Snakes & Ladders The Great British Social Mobility Myth, the gradual climb up the ladder is sometimes undertaken across many generations, with hard graft, luck and much sacrifice, whereas the slide down the snake can happen in an instant, cruelly snatching the rug from beneath you when you least expect it.

Changing your financial situation through Solopreneurship can feel like an insurmountable mountain, with it almost inevitably leading to some kind of slip up, or a running out of fuel for the journey.

Very few of us go into it with our eyes open enough to the pitfalls

Maybe the summit of the mountain, the goal of financial freedom (whatever that means) isn't the goal, maybe one of the smaller mountains is enough, maybe the slower easier route is the better strategy for you.

The most important thing is we don't end up injured in the process.

## THE SLIPPERY SLOPE OF DOOM

There are some ways for getting a foothold to better protect you as you climb.

But first let's take a quick look at some of the factors that contribute to the slippery slope of financial instability in business...

1. Lack of Financial Goals: Without clear financial goals, individuals may find it difficult to stay motivated to save, invest, and grow their wealth, which can lead to financial instability over time.
2. Lack of Budgeting: Poor financial planning, not taking enough notice of money in and money out makes it easy to overspend, which can lead to debt and, if you leave your head in the sand for too long, potentially even bankruptcy.
3. Living Beyond Your Means: This occurs when someone spends more money than they earn. It's a dangerous path that often leads to financial crisis or never being able to build wealth. This can include high-interest credit card debt, or other forms of non-strategic debt.

4. No Emergency Fund: Without an emergency savings pot or insurance, people are often forced to take on debt to cover these unforeseen expenses, which can lead to financial instability. If you rely on your business income to support your lifestyle, what would happen if you couldn't work?
5. Failing to Save for Retirement: Without adequate retirement savings, individuals may find themselves broke in their later years when income sources are limited, and they may have other challenges like caring for offspring and parents, and maybe even managing health issues.
6. Poor Investment Choices: Investing in risky ventures and partnerships without proper knowledge or diversification can result in financial losses. This can also include financial abuse and manipulation... or simply a bad choice of romantic partner.

Which of these are your nemesis? Which would give you the most freedom if you addressed it once and for all this year? Is there someone else in your life, who struggles with any of the above, which has a knock-on effect to your life?

Then there are totally unexpected issues like job loss, contracts coming to an end, and on a larger scale, war, famine, economic downturns, cost of living crisis...oh and a global bloody pandemic.

And so, when you look at all of this, it is easy to see how solopreneurs on the never-ending roller coaster of feast and famine in business, can be further affected by these challenges... and we find ourselves in that attitude of "When the business is doing better, I will sort all of that out"

But will you?

How do we start addressing these things NOW? How do we better protect ourselves? How do we embed better habits and behaviours around creating first and foremost safety and security, and then secondly freedom and abundance.

Before we even start to think about how to make more money, or leveraging our existing resources, we must take a look at your greatest untapped asset.

YOU.

You as a solopreneur
You as a human
You as the leader of your own life and business

It starts with assessing your unique capabilities, your unique story, your make up, literally what's in your DNA.

Now this is not just about your personal brand, or how you show up in the world, but it is about how you choose to grow your business for maximum impact ...because the truth is there isn't a business strategy that suits all, hence the plethora of business gurus out there, all saying "Pick me, Pick me!".

In the next chapter you will hear about how we apply learning so that it works for our particular set of circumstances, and that starts with doing some self-reflection, and then putting reminders in place, so that you truly leverage your assets.

Recap...What is an asset?

**Asset: A useful or valuable thing, person, or quality. In financial terms, it's something that has measurable value that can be converted into cash. It can however increase and decrease in value over time and can also be subjective.**

Quite often we don't even truly understand what assets we have available to us, and I like to think of them as interchangeable with resources, because we can cash them in so to speak.

You might think of business assets as

- Stock if you sell physical items
- Computers and equipment
- Tech systems
- Your email list (great asset btw)
- Your staff or freelance team
- Your website
- Your intellectual property (protected or otherwise)

Assets should bring wealth, especially when you stack them and leverage them to acquire more. It is that acquisition of assets that builds value over time... and yet so often we undervalue our assets and they then lose value.

You are your greatest asset

When we are on the struggle bus in business it is hard to think about yourself as an asset, and you may go as far as thinking of yourself as a liability... i.e. the business would be amazing if someone else could just come and run it for you.

However, being broke... or should I say having limited access to money combined with your personal story of struggle can be your greatest asset, think of all of the other people who have used their rocky starts to build great empires.

In the book The Power of Broke, author Daymond John (founder of clothing brand FUBU and TV judge from the American business show Shark Tank) encourages us to embrace our constraints and be fuelled by them, he says:

*"Being broke can be your super-power, the thing that makes you realize who you are, what you want and how to get it. Being broke*

*doesn't just make you hungry to succeed; it makes you smarter in the face of adversity."*

And he should know, he went from sweeping floors to becoming an investor with an estimated net worth of $350 Million... and has never hidden his story of struggle and hardship.

One of the things which holds solopreneurs back the most is the fear of judgement, the fear of being compared to others in their niche, the fear of not having anything unique to bring to the table.

How can I possibly add value to people's lives if my life isn't totally figured out? Sound familiar?

I include myself in this.

When I first started delivering business coaching it was to existing clients who were inspired by what I had done in my running business, and that was fine. They already knew and trusted me... but I held myself back when it came to getting in front of new audiences.

I was worried that I didn't have enough credentials compared to some of the bigger more well-established online business coaches. I worried I didn't have credibility as a coach because I hadn't reached 7 figures... despite having consulted and worked on projects and programmes that had in fact generated such numbers.

But when I spotted my clients having similar wobbles, I knew I had to create a tool to unpack what it is that makes us all unique.

I call it EQEQ

E - Experience - What you have done to get you to this point in business?

This means ALL of it, don't just consider the stuff that you think is relevant to what you are doing now. I used to only use my example of growing my global fitness business as evidence of credibility. But before that I worked on the engagement policy for 70,000 games makers for the London 2012 Olympics. Why does that matter? No other business coach to my knowledge has that experience of mass engagement and planning for legacy... it might not be in the online coaching world, but the skillset and passion are totally transferable.

Q - Qualifications - What qualifies you to do this work?

This is not just about your official qualifications. I have a degree in performing arts and a masters in multimedia so my creative side helps people unlock ideas in a way that other business coaches might not be able to. What also qualifies me is my life-long commitment to change and transformation.

E - Expertise what are you really skilled in that you are not utilising

You might have a knack for something that you have never trained in. I am an inspiring speaker and activator; I can get folks excited about things and bring them on a journey with me. I've spent 20 years building communities, online and offline, with a speciality in working with hard-to-reach groups

Q - Quirks - What are the qualities you have that you think are not appropriate or relevant to business

I am funny as hell (award winning stand up I will have you know), and I have been able to use this humour in my speaking and writing to great effect, I have also used this with clients to make their content more impactful. I'm a massive empath, my friends call me tiny tears and my clients love these things about me.

Some people choose to work with me because I am from East London, because I am a single mum, because I am a proud ally for underrepresented groups, because I am no bullshit in my approach... these things stand me apart.

Now these things alone are probably not enough to generate success but understanding them and creating a personal brand and a business that utilises all these facets, means you will stand out, and you will spend less time second guessing yourself.

The thing is these qualities are still subjective... and I am a massive fan of using existing diagnostic tools that others will recognise, for example

- Human Design... manifesting generator here
- Wealth Dynamics... star, creator here
- DISC... High Influence, followed by Dominance...almost no compliance lol
- Numerology... my master number is a 55

Now the above will only mean something if you have also used these tools.

They have, each in their own way over the years, helped me to have a better understanding of myself, what drives me, my behaviours, my personality, my tenancies, my destiny (particularly in terms of the numerology stuff) ... and how best to show up in business.

But over and above all of these I would recommend the Clifton Strength Finder Assessment (I wish I was an affiliate for this tool, as I get many of my clients to do this test ha ha)

The way this tool works is it helps you identify your top 10 strengths

When I worked with a Strengths Coach during a high growth period in my business some years back, I literally cried when I got the results back. I felt seen for the first time. I felt validated. I felt like the things I believed I was strong at, I now had evidence to back it up.

My Top 10 Strengths are...

1. Ideations
2. Activator
3. Futuristic
4. Woo (winning others over not spiritual woo)
5. Significance
6. Strategic
7. Command
8. Focus
9. Input
10. Communication

Yours will be different, as there are 34 in total, giving you a unique DNA of your distinct set of talents. Consistency, harmony, discipline... all feature quite low on my list, so I have to use tech, tools and other people to build this into my business, otherwise there would be total chaos.

Can you see how a tool like this would inform the way you run your business? Can you see how looking at these regularly would bring you back from trying things completely out of your zone of genius?

I use this list almost daily.

I do the top 5 intuitively now, as I have been leaning into those since I did the test 4 years ago, the bottom 5 I work a little harder to implement, I pause and ask myself "am I communicating this in the best way?" "Am I being strategic enough?"... which stops me from heading off with every genius idea to grow my business which can lead to all kinds of trouble.

Diagnostic tools only work however, if you take the learning and implement the suggested actions, and also keep them front of mind.

And finally... a word on niching... you know that thing ALL the business coaches say you need to do before you can make any money; it involves finding AND leveraging your uniquely awesome sauce so that people want to do business with you and only you.

For many years I have run a FREE programme called Nail Your Niche with literally hundreds of small business owners taking part, some with AMAZING success, defining their niche and using that to exponentially grow their business, but others seemed to get in their own head about choosing a niche... reluctant to move forward until they did.

You can't waste time on this stuff.

Sometimes you just have to work with what you have and let your niche, your brand voice, your identity as a business owner evolve over time, so if you are not clear on yours, pick something give yourself 6 months, and see where it takes you.

I have done a million things across my career, my portfolio career, my roller coaster, soap opera of a life... and you know, all that experience, all those different sectors, settings and setbacks enrich my knowledge and understanding of the world.

Ultimately I am my niche.

Ultimately you are your niche.

You do not need some complicated equation to help you work out a snazzy elevator pitch, however, if every time someone asks what you do, you spit out any old rubbish or worse, take 25 minutes to explain it because you know it's complicated and you wear many hats.

You will miss out on opportunities.

The truth is people don't give a shit about your hats, or the fancy way in which you describe yourself. What they really care about is whether you can do something for them or maybe if they can do something for you. They are looking for connection, they want to understand what box to put you in, so don't leave it to other people do all the hard work, folks are lazy and busy, and they will move on if you make it too hard for them to get it.

When in doubt do you, do you but with all the bells and whistles

As my good friend Dolly Parton says,

*"Find out who you are and do it on purpose"*

As we move through the book I will remind you time and time again that you are your greatest asset, everything you need to be successful and wealthy you already have inside of you... the trouble is in

A. Believing that
B. Leveraging it effectively

Plus, get this self-worth stuff even remotely right, and you start to impact on that repeating cycle, you start to repair the generational wounds of lack, you give hope and inspiration to future generations, and become an amazing role model to those around you who can pick up the baton and continue this important work.

No pressure lol

### How NOT to be Broke Top Tip

We often forget what assets we have, what resources we have available to us. Tools, techniques, courses, materials, worksheets, concepts... all things we might use if we only remembered to.

I use Trello as a tool for keeping tabs on all my assets. I have developed a CEO dashboard which is easily adaptable for all types of business owners. It acts as HQ for all my important data...like links and processes, but also acts as a living breathing business strategy.

I include reminders about what makes me me...my Clifton Strengths, my DISC style, my drivers, my goals, my mission and my WHY.

I check in with this at the start of each week, and then as and when I need to.

Create your own CEO Dashboard, or come and grab one of my templates from www. juliecreffield.com/broke

**Education (n.)**

1530s, "child-rearing," also "the training of animals," from French education (14c.) and directly from Latin *educationem* (nominative *educatio*) "a rearing, training," noun of action from past-participle stem of *educare* (see educate) Originally of instruction in social codes and manners; meaning "systematic schooling and training for work" is from 1610s.

CHAPTER 4

# *EDUCATION + INSIGHT + ACTIVATION = POWER*

***Knowledge is the precursor for power. When combined with action, and intention it becomes real power. But for any of that to work you must have an incredible amount of insight as to who you are, and what it is you are trying to achieve.***

Start with educating yourself on financial literacy and doing daily work on your money mindset, but most importantly take steps to implement what you've learned every damn day. Reading about investing is one thing; actually investing is where the power lies... even if you make mistakes.

I like to think of failure as a type of tuition fee for the most critical form of learning, and the sooner you pay the fee, the earlier you can make the adjustments and never need to reinvest in the same way.

I used to think that education alone was power, if I took formal education as far as I could, and learned a bit about what the rich people already knew about money and success, then I would somehow make it in life and escape the relative poverty and barriers I was born into.

It came as a bit of a surprise when I realised that there was more to it than that, and that education, although important, was not enough alone. I had to learn about some of the structural inequalities that were making it harder for people like me. Oh, and nobody told me that the goal posts would keep moving, and that I would have to be on top of my education on an ongoing basis.

Do you remember when you first learned about money?

Was it at school in maths, or was it at home when the tooth fairy paid a visit? Did you have a money box, a building society account, or maybe even a trust fund? Did you have play money, did you get an allowance, were you told no when you asked for things in the shop, or did you always get the items you asked for on your Xmas list?

The things is, most of us don't get a formal education around money, we learn about it instead through the day-to-day use of money, predominantly by the adults in our lives, and then bit by bit we are given more responsibility to look after our own money.

These days kids are influenced by what they see on the TV, and on social media, lifestyle content and advertising specifically used to activate desire and consumerism from an early age.

But that's not wealth, right?

Not really? Surely it goes beyond that.

There was no financial education to speak of back in the early 90's for girls like me.

Remember education was still relatively new for working class girls. And NO, I am not a total ancient relic. Secondary education became compulsory in the UK with the Education Act of 1944, that's just 30 odd years, two generations, before I was born.... my Nan left school at 11, my Mum completed secondary school and went straight into the workforce as a secretary for a bank, I was the first EVER to go into higher education in my family.

The education act laid the groundwork for the modern comprehensive education system as we know it and marked a significant step towards providing accessible and compulsory free education for all children, regardless of their social background.

Many of the female teachers from my school would have used the short burst of opportunity that came after the 2$^{nd}$ world war to move up the social and economic ladder, with the increase in working class people having access to further and higher education, AND the increased need for teachers, social workers and government officials.

Teaching as a profession was a viable option for smart people from the lower classes and I wonder how much that shaped the curriculum, or the teaching of the curriculum and the views that the teachers had on what we would be capable of.

In the first two years of school, we had to do Home Economics, which was not about the cost of running a home; it was instead about baking cakes and laying a table so it looked nice for your husband when he got home from work. Like REALLY? Oh, and needlework. Let's not forget the needlework.

What if I wanted to do woodwork, or business studies? Subjects that my brother was able to take at his school in the late 80's? It wasn't fair and I knew it, even back then.

I found school a total contradiction. I loved to learn, I was bright, and liked the structure, but I somehow found it hard to follow the rules and would often get in trouble for nothing more than speaking my mind. How dare I question something a teacher was teaching, how dare I call out unfairness, or ask for an explanation about why rules from over 100 years ago were still in place at the school.

I literally tapped out of GCSE Sociology in week 3 when a teacher shut me down after I questioned a theory...if you couldn't debate a theory in sociology where the hell could you?

One of my finest moments came just 2 years later, when I waved my GCSE results paper in front of his face with my proud B mark, and in amazement he said *"How the fuck did you manage that Creffield"* to which I responded,

*"Sociology sir, it's about life innit... maybe you should go get yourself one"* before strutting off with my friends, forgetting I would be back after the summer holidays, as I was doing a Drama BTEC at the schools mixed 6$^{th}$ form.

Teachers labelled me as a trouble-maker, and maybe I was.

My Drama teacher took a liking to me though, she didn't mind my attitude, nor did my form teacher Miss Gleeson, who was also my English teacher for the last two years of my school life, she could see I had a knack for storytelling, and a love of books.

What I now know is that I had undiagnosed ADHD, which accounted for my lack of concentration in subjects like maths, science and languages, and yet hyper focus in subjects I enjoyed like English, Religious Education, and drama where I over performed.

I was also dealing with the breakdown of my mum and dad's marriage, and life at home was chaotic. None of those things were taken into consideration, and I heard the messages loud and clear that I was too much, and yet not enough at the same time. I was the problem. I wasn't working hard enough. I was unlikely to become anything of substance.

Selina Todd the British historian known for her research on the working class and women's history in the 20th century talks about the role of education in shaping social mobility and class dynamics.

"Education and training don't create opportunity, but they do determine who is able to take advantage of it."

Nobody ever imagined I would go to university.

It was only really the girls in Strasburg who were encouraged to think about higher education... yes, in Year 9 our school classes were renamed after European cities, which was an improvement I guess from the biblical names they originally were.

I was told that I wasn't academic despite being in Rouen, just one set below the top set, and yet I went on to get a first class degree with honours. I then went on to do a masters in multimedia, design and culture... and one day I'm sure I will do a PHD.

Educating oneself about wealth involves understanding not just how money works, but also the principles, mindsets, and strategies that can lead to financial prosperity, and these are forever evolving, especially in a business context.

There are various ways to educate yourself about wealth:

- Books
- Online Courses
- Blogs & Websites
- Seminars & Workshops
- Podcasts
- Financial Planners & Advisors
- Networking/Masterminds
- Mentorship & Incubators
- Universities & Community Colleges
- Documentaries & Movies
- Apps & Tools
- Magazines & Newspapers

But here's the thing, sometimes the best education comes from trying things out for yourself. Learning through doing. Start small, like investing a small amount in stocks or starting a side-business, and learn from your experiences.

As with any educational journey, it's essential to maintain a critical mindset. Not all advice will be relevant or useful for your specific situation. Always do your own research and consider consulting with professionals before making significant financial decisions.

The age of selling information to hungry learners is almost over, let's face it there probably isn't a thing on this planet that you couldn't learn with hyper focus, an internet connection, and a library card. It is all about implementation now, and deciphering what learning is relevant.

This starts with knowing what kind of business you are running, what that means in terms of creating an income generation strategy for that business, and the opportunities and limitations of each option.

I never forget reading Rich Dad, Poor Dad for the first time and realising I never had a single person in my family that I could talk to about money. Having a mentor to explain to you how to leverage your wealth, how to avoid the traps that so many people, employed and self -employed, make when it comes to creating wealth is invaluable, so if you can, go find someone to have those conversations with.

We can't rely on just our parents anyway... the world is changing fast, and unless they are where you want to be, they might not be able to give sound advice anyway. My parents bought their first house for £11,000.... you can't buy a decent car for that now. Home ownership isn't viable for so many young people, especially those living in big expensive cities like London.

So how do we build wealth?

Rich Dad Poor Dad Author, Robert Kiyosaki, says its simple:

*"The poor and middle classes work for money, the rich have money work for them"*

That takes some getting your head around. It also takes some real strength and courage, not to look at that and say, *"Well that's me fucked then".* So many of the structures at play, capitalism, white privilege, classism, patriarchy...they are literally designed to keep the status quo happily in place.

But things are changing, in part because the internet has opened opportunities for us to learn about wealth creation, and there are amazing influencers and educators out there shining a light on the inequalities that exist, and what we can do to collectively address them.

The premise of Roberts book, Rich Dad Poor Dad is that the rich and the poor have different mindsets and different behaviours, and that in turn allows them different allowances and opportunities. I mean, we know that right?

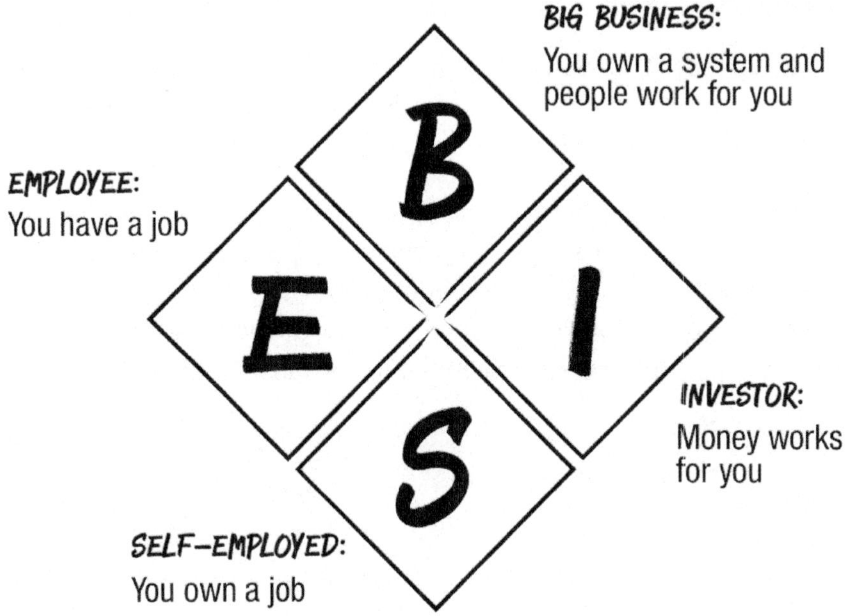


In his Cashflow Quadrant graphic you can see he breaks it down to Small Business, Big Business, Employed and Investors...who all make their money in different ways.

The thing which struck me most when I read this book over a decade ago was the difference between small business (the solopreneur) and big business. The small business owner owns a job...the big business owns a system, a system that can be leveraged, repeated, tweaked for productivity and profit...and ultimately has other people doing most of the work.

Now you might not want other people working for you... trust me, I know, I am not the greatest at managing others either. But even knowing the different opportunities and challenges these two differing business types presents puts you at an advantage. This enables you to create a business growth strategy that is aligned to your skills set and your ambition for the scale and form of your growing venture AND it makes you a more discerning consumer of training and coaching too.

You know how I said mistakes are like tuition fees for growth and learning. The same can be true for bad investments in learning, it's like a growth tax...one I am no longer willing to pay each year.

I have "invested" more than £100,000 in online coaches, and programmes to help support my business growth journey. This has been out of the revenue created from my business and over an 8-year period... so does not include my formal education but does include my coaching qualification which felt like a sensible thing to invest in at the time.

Did those investments pay off?

Yes and no.

When you are in the market for coaching or even when you are not, you are easily manipulated by powerful marketing to believe that -XYZ programme- will be the thing that unlocks your success.

Once you get into the marketing pipeline of these companies (or individuals), it's almost a done deal that at some point you will buy from them, unless you have really clear boundaries and can spot the marketing and sales tactics from a mile off.

These coaches use these tactics because they work. I have used them in the past because they work.

When you learn about sales and influence and get underneath the buying psychology that prompts us all to say YES, you become more empowered both as a seller and as a consumer, and then you can start asking better quality questions.

I didn't always ask the right questions.

All 5 of the mentors/coaches I worked with over that 8 year period had a system, a system that left you always wanting and needing more coaching and support from them, and always at a higher price point.

Some examples...

I did a year of amazing group coaching with someone to get my head around marketing and keeping things simple in my business. The following year the model changed, the cost of the mastermind went up whilst the access to the coach went down, and the group then became led by one of my peers (a previous participant) who's business expertise was around the same level of mine... I respectfully withdrew from that programme.

The following year I worked with 2 coaches from the states, BIG investments and in-person retreats. They were amazing, they helped me up my game, and understand the global possibilities for my brand... and it did wonders for my profile, but there was always something else to buy, another level to unlock... the minute you leave you are dead to them lol.

I remember at one retreat that I had paid $7000 dollars to attend, on the 5$^{th}$ day they started seeding the next thing, a $50,000 investment, and on the final evening they laid on a party with free booze, and all their staff team having strategic conversations, order forms in hand.

They nearly got me...nearly.

Now you get to decide whether these practices are ethical or not. Who knows what that $50,000 investment might have unlocked in me... the thing is though, it might not have led to anything, other than a $50,000 hole in my accounts... and nobody ever asked me about my ability to spend that much.

They always say though: *"if you want it enough, you will find a way"*

What I know is at the higher levels of business, I have heard time and time again gurus state *"Yeah I know only 1% will ever get the success, but hey that's the system, that's the way it works"*

Results cannot be promised, they simply can't... there are too many variables.

When I was running my Tribe Builder programme of which around 200 solopreneurs went through, for sure I had clients who went from low key coaches and experts, to business owners with huge followings and multiple income streams off the back of their involvement, I still watch them grow years on, proud that I played a small part in it.

But I also had people who didn't want to go so big, couldn't find the hook, had visibility issues, or family crises, or not enough time to implement the strategies. I am still their cheerleader though, I still watch with interest to see how they are doing.

It was never the case of,

*"They just didn't want it enough"* or *"They didn't have what it takes"*

Some coaching relationships can be damaging. Some high-ticket offers are plain and simply cons. The quality of the learning is no different to what you can find on a more affordable programme, or for free or low cost online or in books, it's just that gurus need to charge that much to differentiate themselves, to pay their large teams, and to cover their huge Facebook marketing costs.

I invested around £25,000 in one coach over around a 3-year period.

My business went from inconsistent £3-£6K months, to consistent £10K months, and then 6-figure launches, and ultimately my best year in business. I learned a lot on that programme, through the coaches approach, being in a space with other ambitious business owners, and the accountability that comes with making an investment like that.

The programme did what it was supposed to for me... but it didn't for everyone, and the relationship with the coach didn't end well.

Something I had said in an online event about my results was used out of context and without my permission, used as a public testimonial in her marketing, I pulled the coach up on it because what I had said in the constraints of that event had included references to both my daughter and her dad, and she didn't have their consent to share, even if in the small print of the event sign up she had mine.

I was totally gaslit over the complaint and told that I still had healing work to do... which feels like the original piss take, an awful abuse of trust in the client coach relationship... as I had disclosed super personal things while under hypnosis with that coach which is what she was referring to.

Trust and respect is everything in a coaching relationship.

She totally lost mine.

Now you might think I would have learned my lesson, and would avoid high profile coaches, but the thing is I am still a fan of working with external coaches, educators and mentors, and I am not afraid to invest at a higher level. I know personally that accountability and being in community with businesses at a similar level really works for me.

I just know better what to look for now, what questions to ask, what I personally need.

I went on to work with one further high profile coach, more of a school of coaches, an approach rather than an individual, although it was still headed up by an individual, a bloke this time, and I was miss sold right from the off.

I already had a multi 6 figure business at this point, and was interested in joining their 7 figure mastermind. I had had my best year in business off the back of the Covid pandemic, and I was at that time (possibly as a hangover from working with the previous coach) still on a "who wants to be a millionaire" trajectory.

I was convinced to join the lower tier of their programme, to get some of my back end things in place. At this point I was still flying solo, and the head guy felt like without some of the systems in place I might struggle in the smaller but much more advanced business group, despite my clear ability to sell.

It made sense. Until it didn't.

The mastermind I joined was not actually a mastermind, the group literally had hundreds of participants and the content was very similar to stuff I had already learned and implemented in my business, but trying not to be discouraged as he had clearly said I could move up as soon as it made sense, I focussed on getting my systems in order, I hired a part time business manager, did a few successful launches and then requested to move up for more of a stretch.

I was told no.

So, despite having invested £18,000 in a programme that was wrong for me, and willing to pay even more to be in the right room, I was actually laughed at, almost like he didn't believe my turnover. My belief is that my original coach who I had fallen out with the previous year was in that higher level mastermind, so it was a conflict of interest. When I asked for a refund for part of the £18,000 as I didn't see any value in staying in the container for the rest of the year, again I was laughed at, and told that's not how it works.

Turns out there is literally an online support group for people who have been on that very same programme, and have left with no tangible results. I am not sure that knowing you were not the only one that got burned makes you feel more or less of a victim... that company is still very much out there targeting the people who have the dream of business success and have close to £20,000 to throw at it.

Those were very expensive, painful lessons.

Now remember, this is only my take on these interactions.

Maybe I need to take more responsibility for the role I played. Maybe I should have done more due diligence, maybe I didn't ask the right questions, maybe I didn't follow enough of their advice, maybe I didn't have what it takes to scale to a million.

Ultimately those coaches taught me how I want to do business as a coach and strategist, but also what lengths I need to go to as a consumer of coaching, mentoring and support moving forward to keep myself safe.

I include these stories not because I am malicious or jealous, or want people to stop investing in coaches. I share these stories because many of these interactions almost broke me. Financially, emotionally, spiritually and physically... I literally had physical responses to each of these interactions....by emitting these stories I wouldn't be sharing the whole picture.

I sometimes wonder if the coaching industry in itself makes people feel more broke than they actually are, picking at wounds, finding niggles, uncovering things we hadn't even thought about before.

And yet personal development has been a guiding light for me, and for so many others that I know.

But I have had friends, peers and clients come to me in tears after investing huge amount of money on programmes that haven't worked out. Folks who have re-mortgaged their homes, borrowed money without partners knowing, run themselves into the ground trying to recover some of the costs.

I want people to be more decerning in their education. I do not want to further add to the mystery of what it takes to grow in the online business world.

It takes time to recover from these interactions, no matter how tough your skin is. We build relationships with these people, these influencers, these gurus, who pull us in with their messages of hope (remember people, hope is NOT a strategy) and they talk to us like they are our friends, our peers.

They are not.

When I was hospitalised with COVID in October 2021 not one of those 5 individuals wished me well, out of hundreds and hundreds of messages of support, despite all of them still being contacts across my social media, their silence spoke volumes.

I know I played a role in making some bad investing decisions, and I feel terrible that I used money that I could have taken out of my business and used to move me and my daughter Rose out of East London sooner.

In Chapter 5 I will share with you a way of investigating the kind of business you want to grow so that you can make more informed decisions when you are buying in support to do that... because having mentors is an amazing way to grow a business, but finding the right kind of mentor is critical.

For now, I'd just say be careful where you get your education from... ask yourself - what are they REALLY selling and what is the cost to me, especially if I am NOT in the 1%? Do you need to learn more, understand more, or simply implement what you already know more?

Choose your support accordingly.

The truth is for far too long we have got caught up in the proposition of social mobility, the ability to climb up the social and economic ladder through education, talent and hard work; You can be the absolute BEST at what you do in your business, but if some one else is better at marketing and has access to funds to drive traffic, then they will totally out sell you...and that is just a fact.

Some people get into positions of power and authority not because they are best, not because they have worked the hardest, but because they had money to play with, they had the right connections, they were in the right place at the right time.

This is true as much in politics, and formal education as it is in business... these gurus might say they care about fairness, they might have social causes that they publicly support, but they and their teams can still use terrible business practices and be a total dick.

Not everything you read online is true...including those income claims.

If you want to be more powerful as a solopreneur and go after what you want, then remember...

Education + Insight + Activation = Power

Power to drive change
Power to drive profit
Power to fight for equality

It is a complex world out there. There are some amazing coaches, educators, activators, creators and mentors to support the Education

+ Insight + Activation equation.... so, seek them out, and always do your due diligence.

REMEMBER...Radical Self-responsibility.

Nobody is coming to save you, you don't need rescuing, you can be your own hero.

Plus.. forgive yourself for all of your "not knowing", we make decisions with the information we have available to us at the time. When we know better, we do better right? Forgive and move on...that includes letting go of the anger towards anyone you think has done you dirty with money...holding onto it just keeps you stuck, and we need movement where we are going.

Forgive just don't forget lol

It starts with educating yourself, looking inwards so you get the insight, and then it requires action, sustained, messy, fast and inspired action... knowing you will make mistakes, and that those mistakes will further support your learning and understanding of *How NOT to be Broke*.

### How NOT to be Broke Top Tip

Make a list of all the formal qualifications and certifications you have, then include the skills you have acquired, and the experience and expertise that sets you apart from others in your industry.

Think about all the books you have read, the courses you have taken, and the learning curves you have been on to upskill yourself when it comes to technology, process and systems.

Where are you leaving money on the table by NOT implementing what you know?

Where could you get more of a competitive edge, and show your expertise by talking more about your formal and non-formal education, and the skills and experience you acquired through implementation?

Then write a list of all your REAL and PERCIEVED knowledge gaps, try not to include new areas of work to add to your current skillset (more strings to your bows), but structural things which are holding you back from business growth because you don't understand them.

Allocate an amount of time (and money) for education in this area only... and don't use procrasta-learning as an excuse for not doing the stuff you know works...like marketing and sales, and getting in front of new audiences.

**audit (n.)**

early 15c., "official examination of accounts," from Latin *auditus* "a hearing, a listening," past participle of *audire* "to hear" (from PIE root au "to perceive"). Official examination of accounts originally was an oral procedure. The word also formerly was used in a sense of "official audience, judicial hearing or examination" (1590s).

CHAPTER 5

# MEASURE THE METRICS THAT MATTER

***Track your financial progress like your life depends on it. This means monitoring your income, expenses, savings, and investments. Look at the other metrics that matter to you too. Understanding how these numbers interplay with one another provides clarity on your financial health and guides you in making informed choices.***

This is the chapter of the book you probably want to skip, as it is the part of the CEO role that many business owners want to, and choose to, omit from their working week. However, I can't stress enough how critical it is to you not being or ending up broke as a solopreneur...so skip it at your peril.

Having an accountant or a bookkeeper or even a financial director in your business is fine to drive some of this work, if you prefer to outsource some of this stuff, but not knowing what's going on with your money, and the other metrics that drive wealth in your business and in your life, well that responsibility I am afraid is down to you.

In the early stages of my business in the early 2000's, when I set up Urban 8 Creative Solutions (my first consultancy business) a lovely man from the tax office came round to my house and he explained the ins and outs of how tax worked.

I felt both stupid and grown up at the same time as my mum busied herself in the kitchen so as not to disturb us... and it was particularly exciting when he told me I could offset some of my tax bill with expenses such as stationery... did someone say stationery?

But my business was simple then. I had set up a company to protect me, but I was in effect a sole trader, a freelancer, someone trading their time for money...and I didn't have many expenses as I was back living with my mum after graduating, and she was still charging just £300 a month for bed and board.

I had a day rate which ranged from £150-£450 depending on how cheeky I could be and what I could get away with...and my only real outgoings were travel expenses and the occasional trip to WHSmith's... yes this was long before Paperchase and Amazon came along.

I would go on to mix full time employment with my training and consultancy work for 10 years, enjoying holidays, clothes, and nights out, even managing to save money for a deposit for a flat in Stratford... gosh you couldn't do that now.

A whole decade later, when I started my online business, things felt more complicated. I had purchased an iMac computer with some of my income, advised by my accountant, a local fella who came to my apartment once every few months to remind me to keep better records.

But now all sorts of other expenses, income, and expenditure were being added to the business model. I had merchandise; I was hosting events; I was purchasing tech to run the back end of the website; print costs; it was hard to keep a track of it all.

I had the added pressure of juggling complicated, and quite frankly unfair, personal expenses now too, as a new mum covering most of the household bills, childcare costs, and the bullshit that is the family tax credit system.

Spreadsheets hurt my head, the idea of creating a budget seemed silly as I didn't feel like I could predict income because the business was always seeming to be up against new challenges and opportunities, and so I just winged it.

Until that was one year when my tax bill came and at the same time I was simultaneously asked to pay back a massive whack of family tax credit. I felt completely broken by all the effort I had gone to for so little reward. I realised that I wasn't left with anything at the end of the year, and other than the bare minimum I took out to cover my living costs, I was just about breaking even.

From the outside I looked successful, a familiar story for so many mums in business, and in the workplace, especially in the early years when childcare costs literally fuck you over. You should be doing better... but it feels like the world is conspiring against you all the time.

It wasn't that I couldn't make money or grow my business. My profile, my audience, my confidence, had all come on leaps and bounds. I just couldn't understand where all the revenue was going, or which of my products and services were even profitable.

I had multiple streams of income

- Digital Products
- Courses
- Merchandise
- Events
- Sponsorship Deals

- Paid speaking gigs
- Book royalties

But it never seemed enough to buy in the help I needed, or to take money out of the business to go on holiday or move out of my 2-bed apartment that we were fast outgrowing.

Something needed to change.

It was around this time that I started reading books about money, and there were two books which were pivotal to me (FYI, I have a full list of book recommendations and resources at www.juliecreffield.com/broke)

Get Rich, Lucky Bitch... by Denise Duffield Thomas, and Profit first by Mike Michalowicz

The first helped me understand that how I thought and felt about money, was totally having an impact on my ability to make, keep and leverage it, and the second gave me the biggest kick up the backside ever needed to manage my money properly so that I knew exactly how profitable my business was.

Not only did these books teach me something but they instilled two foundational actions that I have maintained ever since, which led to the start of my financial success in business, leading me to the goal that many solopreneurs aim towards, that of consistent £10K revenue months.

### Action 1 - Tracking income AND value

We often track our expenses but don't track what's coming in and where from.

Denise encourages her readers to track and be grateful for every single penny or cent that comes in. If you can't be grateful for that £10 you made, how will you be grateful for the £100. Same with value, I was getting a lot of freebies back then, and OK, granted I couldn't pay my mortgage with energy drinks, or sports watches but it proved that I was able to attract value and leverage that value into cash.

How this worked is I simply tracked (using an app) every bit of income and value that came into my business and life... in one big pot, but segmented it into income and value obviously, but also into some categories so I could see what the ratio was.

I was attracting a whole heap of wealth, wealth that I was dismissing and not being particularly grateful for.

I started setting the goal of having £10K months around this time too. I didn't hit that goal for well over a year, but having it on my tracker pushed me to think differently about money and how I made it.

£10K months then became my new normal, my non-negotiable.

### Action 2 - Segmenting my Money

The Profit First system is an accounting methodology that turns normal accounting totally on its head. You will have to read the book to truly understand how and why it works (and it's a hard read, especially if you know you are not profitable now), but the thing I took most from it was the segmentation of my income the moment it came into my account... before I got excited and spent it on stationery lol.

What this looks like in practice is having a ratio (a percentage that Mike calls TAPS) that is siphoned into different pots...one for profit (my money) one for tax (the governments money) and one for (contingency) just in case money... the rest I leave for operating costs for recurring bills, expenses and sharpie pens.

This system combined with paying myself twice a month instead of once, forced me to look at my numbers more frequently, and encouraged me to make more offers in my business...we will talk about this in the chapter on sales.

Now, I know how much resistance I had to making these changes, and so I want you to take the pressure off yourself and know that this stuff is a process. Beating yourself up about not having all your ducks in a row, doesn't help anyone... but neither does being in denial about your business and life finances.

It's time to do **The How Not to Be Broke Audit**

Conducting a financial audit as a solopreneur would normally involve reviewing your business finances comprehensively to ensure accuracy, identify any inefficiencies, and gauge your overall financial health.

It might include the following process...

1. Gathering Financial Documents
2. Review Income Streams
3. Audit Expenses
4. Reconcile Bank Statements
5. Review Accounts Receivable
6. Check Accounts Payable
7. Evaluate Debt
8. Analyse Profit and Loss Statement
9. Review Tax Obligations
10. Assess Your Financial Systems
11. Set new Financial Goals
12. Adjust business strategy accordingly

Well, I can tell you... I don't do all of this consistently and rely heavily on my accountant to keep on top of the data, because like many solopreneurs I also don't like having to do the detail level of financial reconciliation blah blah blah.

But I do know my numbers. I know my profit levels. I do know how to grow month-on-month using the data that I collect to drive my strategy. For me though there are other metrics of success that matter beyond revenue and profit, other measurables that drive business growth, and enable wealth creation AND add to my life in ways money alone can't.

I believe it is important that you come up with your own process for tracking data and using it to inform decisions, a process that you are more likely to embrace regularly without that sense of doom.

I call my process the 5 eyes....in other words what do I need to keep an eye on?

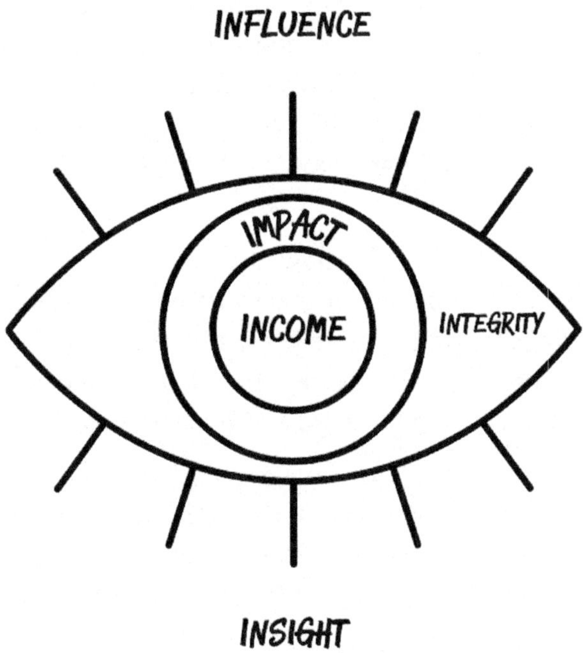


1. Income – How much money have I made this month, from where, and whom? How easy did it feel? How much of it was profit? And what was the cost to my health and happiness from acquiring this income generation?

I also keep an eye on where I may not have made a heap of money, but where the income generating tasks, I did undertake may lead to a return on investment later down the line... this is about understanding your product and services ladder, AND your customers buying journey.

2. Impact – What difference did I make with my business activities this month? Where did the business do good, both for me, my loved ones, my clients and my wider stakeholders? Did I create value for others, that creates a bank of good will. Did I do things that I can leverage, like growing my audience, increasing my reach?
3. Influence – How has my profile or ability to influence my audience increased or decreased over the last month? Where have I featured, which new audiences have I got in front of? Has my reputation improved or been adversely affected by anything? How much power and clout do I have in my industry?
4. Insight – What do I know that I didn't know last month? How am I implementing my learning? Applying my skills and knowledge to create growth? What am I hearing? What developments have happened in my niche or industry. Am I listening to my ideal client and their problems?
5. Integrity – How aligned have my actions been to my values? Have I behaved in alignment with my ethics, or have they been tested in any way. Have I established trust and good will, have I built up my bank of good karma? Have I done what I said I would do

Now these might seem like wishy washy metrics to you. But with these as a guide I can create a series of tangible KPIs that not only track outcomes, but promote action, quite literally prompting me to get out of my own way and do the things that make a difference.

Want to increase your influence? Pitch your story to 3 journalists, or get on 3 podcasts
Want to create more income? Ask for the sale 10 times, raise your prices by 5%
Want more insight? Get your lead generating quiz completed by 30 ideal clients

At the end of the month, you simply need to check in as to whether you did those things or not, then you can measure the impact of those things further down the line. By creating your own metrics that matter, with tangible KPIs you get to hold yourself accountable to the things that matter to you? Plus, you can ramp things up and down as you like.

There are some months where income generation is THE only measurement that matters...it's the difference between putting food on the table and not.

It cannot be the only driver EVERY month surely? That would lead to burnout.

Some months perhaps it needs to be about increasing your influence, which might come at a short-term cost to generating sales... or maybe it is about more insight, time to test something new even if it isn't profitable now, but it will pay off in the long term.

When you follow other people's metrics of success, you lose your sense of direction, you find yourself questioning why you are even bothering

But I didn't have a £30K month this month
I don't have 3 new members joining my team
I don't use Facebook ads to drive traffic to my lead magnet
I don't charge high ticket for my coaching
I don't speak for free at conferences
I am not location independent

My kids don't go to private school
My jeans are from Primark not Prada

Some of the above matter to some people, and to others they have nothing to do with their idea of success or failure. Only you get to decide what is important to you, and the more you communicate that with your audience, the more you will help them to understand you, build trust and inevitably find your people.

It comes down to what you value AND the resources you have available in the first place, to play in the entrepreneurial space.

I had to get up to £10K consistent months ASAP, that need was a gift, as it created urgency, and urgency creates action. There is nothing like an impending or unexpected bill to get you focussed on the job in hand.

We each have drivers that make us take action, sometimes we are driven towards something, like a goal, or an increase in status; some people are more driven away from, away from hardship, away from embarrassment, away from going hungry.

There is no right or wrong, but one problem might be that when the urgency stops...you get the car, or you are no longer worried about the gas bill, that the drivers disappear, and you find it hard to motivate yourself. We will look at what we can do to stay hungry after we have filled the fridge a little later in the book.

For now, I just want you to get comfortable with articulating what it is you want and why, what matters to you and why, what you value over and above money in the bank... and why. The answers to those questions should form the basis for your regular financial/business growth audit...or what I like to call my CEO Metric Review.

As a solopreneur you will work *in* the business and *on* the business.

Month-to-month, week-to-week, day-to-day... shit sometimes even hour-to-hour, your role will change as you take on all manner of tasks in the business. You could, if you had the resources, probably outsource many aspects of that too... but one role you cannot outsource is that of CEO... unless you are building a legacy business, but we will talk about that later.

As CEO it is your job to keep the wheels of the business moving.

You are the master strategist, the driver of the bus...you have to manage the resources of the business (and yourself) to ensure all other roles are effective.

And yet how much time do you clear out of your diary for CEO duties?

Facing up to where you are as a business as a business owner isn't always easy. But the sooner you have those difficult conversations with yourself, and maybe even with your loved ones, the easier you will make your journey.

Also... knowing all this stuff makes it easier for others to help you.

Sometimes new clients will tell me all about their business challenges and when I drill down into the details of what's going on, they can't tell me anything with absolute clarity. They don't know how much they are making or what their expenses are, they don't know how their website is performing, or what their conversion rates are, or which of their products and services has the best results.

Most of us go into business because we love the thing our business does, and we don't want to do all of the other stuff that comes with it, but I am sorry to break it to you...TOUGH...that is business; that is Solopreneurship; that is the price you pay for using your business as a route to wealth and abundance... else you are stuck working for someone else who does all of that for you.

In his popular book The Emyth, Michael E. Gerber says

*"If your business depends on you, you don't own a business—you have a job. And it's the worst job in the world because you're working for a lunatic!"*

Ain't that the truth?

So while your business totally depends on you, at least get yourself organised so that if people do come in to support your growth, you can hand over things with ease because there is method to your madness.

I use my CEO dashboard for all of this.

It includes my monthly Audit, all my important information, and many of the systems and processes I use withing my business. You can get access to a template over at www.juliecreffield.com/broke or simply create your own format for reviewing the metrics that matter for you.

Start with a baseline, and think about the things you want to grow that will lead to wealth

- Email list
- Website visits
- Google Searches
- Word of mouth referrals
- Speaking enquiries
- Social media following
- Social media engagement
- Social media enquires
- Lead magnet conversions
- Sales conversations
- Sales conversions
- Testimonials

You can just track a few of these to start, and then add to them as you get into the swing of it. Over time you will work out which ones lead to business traction and which ones don't...learn to be a geek when it comes to your business data.

Make a commitment to collecting the stats, and then sitting down with them. I do this monthly. The day is blocked out of my schedule for the whole year, with some extra time in December to really reflect on the progress and to set goals for the following year.

Without knowing where you are now, it will be hard for you to strategize moving forward.

I don't want to be broke, and I just want to be rich...are sadly not specific enough for this work my friend. It's all subjective anyway... so let's start getting specific about where we are and where we want to be.

In the next chapter we will start to discuss the feasibility of your goals.

### How NOT to be Broke Top Tip

Add Finance Friday to your calendar... 15-20 minute check in of your financial goals and outcomes. Chase those invoices, make some offers, get a grip on what needs to be done next week to stay on track.

Add a CEO date to the end of the month where you review the 5 Eyes and collect, collate and celebrate your wins based on the data that you collect. Then set your goals for the following month.

Keep on top of your emotional triggers when seeing other people celebrating their measures of success, explore any areas of jealousy or rage, and then ground yourself by remembering what it is you want to achieve from your business, your version of freedom and success.

**privilege (n.)**

mid-12c. "grant, commission" (recorded earlier in Old English, but as a Latin word), from Old French privilege "right, priority, privilege" (12c.) and directly from Latin *privilegium* "law applying to one person, bill of law in favor of or against an individual;" in the post-Augustine period "an ordinance in favor of an individual" (typically the exemption of one individual from the operation of a law), "privilege, prerogative," from *privus* "individual"

CHAPTER 6

# FEED YOURSELF AND YOUR LOVED ONES FIRST

***If you are serious about creating financial security, avoid indulging in luxuries or non-essentials in your business AND life at the expense of catering to your basic needs and those of your dependents first. This means saving a portion of all earned income, ensuring health and well-being, and securing a safety net should things go wrong... it also means using your business income wisely so that you build the kind of business that you REALLY want.***

I see so many people investing in things (with both their time and their money) where there is no guarantee of any return on investment, and the odds are stacked in the favour of the bigger fish who benefit either way from your involvement.

The cost of NOT "feeding you and yours first" is immeasurable, and for many is unrecoverable, causing repercussions far beyond the viability of your business venture. When the shit hits the fan, it is fascinating seeing how quickly those contacts scarper.

In late November 2022 I moved to my dream home in the countryside.

A lifetime of living in East London, a few years away at Uni in Winchester, and then 16 years in my 2-bed apartment slap bang in the centre of Stratford, home of the London 2012 Olympics... I was a city girl at heart.

And then here I was packing all my worldly possessions and moving our life, 40 miles up the road to leafy Hertfordshire, to an 1850s converted barn with my own office, and ensuite bathrooms for the pair of us.

I felt like I had finally "made it", all that hard work had finally paid off.

Moving out of East London had been on my vision board for many years, probably since my break with my daughters Dad. I wanted a fresh start, I wanted more space, I wanted to give Rose a different life to the one I had, where she could see that not everywhere has the challenges that inner cities have.

I guess deep down I also wanted to show off a little and say *"See... told you I could change my life"* to all the haters and neigh sayers who doubted me. I also wanted to come through with my promise to Rose, that we would get a dog once we lived in a house.

It had been a long time coming because as a solopreneur, even a super successful one, being able to get a mortgage felt impossible. If you don't have wealthy parents, a life partner to share the risk with, or a super healthy savings pot so you can just buy cash... homeownership as a solopreneur is a total ball ache.

Pop star Lily Allen sung about this on her first record back in 2006 around the same time I was trying to get my first mortgage,

*"I wanna get a flat and know I can afford it*

*It's just the bureaucrats that won't give me a mortgage*

*It's funny because I've got young fucking money*

*But I'm never gonna get it just cos of my bad credit"*

The pandemic, and the UK's cladding issue, added further complications to me selling my apartment in East London and I was now starting to question what freedom being a home owner was actually giving me anyway.

Was it even worth it?

When Robert T. Kiyosaki first published Rich Dad, Poor Dad in 1997 he was criticised for saying a person's house is NOT an asset. I mean that's what our parents had told us right?

*"Get on the property ladder"* it's the only way to get on in the world.

And I had followed that advice.

The pressure to pay my mortgage every month over the past seventeen years, through five redundancies and other hardships in my life, has kept me connected to the goal of making consistent income, but owning that property has also kept me trapped.

I couldn't afford to save much, I didn't have enough income from the business to get a big enough mortgage to buy a house anywhere I wanted to live in London, and my connection to East London was so strong, so in truth I was just scared to make the move.

It didn't feel safe, especially with all the economic uncertainty.

When I was offered a job with a 6-figure salary doing business consulting but just at a higher level, AND with shares in the company, this felt like a smart strategic move.

I remember emailing my mortgage advisor who had a few months prior said' "We could probably get you to somewhere close to £400K with the bumper year you had last year...but it will still be tight" and when I told him about the potential new job he said, "Great news, with that salary, we are talking probably somewhere close to £700K"

It changed EVERYTHING.

And so, I made the move. Luckily, I decided to rent not buy, knowing that this was a BIG decision and I wanted to test run the new area I had chosen for myself, and I still had to sell my flat in Stratford. One small blessing, before the shit hit the fan.

I moved in to "The Barn" at the end of November, had the most amazing family Xmas with Rose and a 7 foot real tree, joined by some of my siblings and nieces and nephews...and of course Tom my ginger cat, who now had acres and acres of farm land to explore.

And then at the end of December I stopped getting paid by my new employer.

In one fell swoop my safety and security was whipped out from beneath me, and I knew I had made a massive error in judgement. I felt physically sick... in fact in January I ended up having a terrible chest infection... literal pain in my heart area, the wind taken out of my sails so to speak.

I felt like such a fraud, like I had somehow imagined this great opportunity, like I was playing make believe with my new life in the countryside. All those voices of "I told you so" and "Why did you need somewhere so flashy" started popping into my head.

I was in some kind of parallel universe, seeing this all play out and not having any control over what was happening. Eventually I encouraged my employer to make me redundant, as the non-payment went on for 3 months... each month with me getting into more and more debt (something I had always avoided), each month getting more and more stressed about my situation.

I had wound down both of my online businesses, to throw everything at this new job. The move had kept me distracted too, as I revelled in the task of furnishing my new house, picking out sofas and rugs, and really making the place feel like home.

I had two months of absolute bliss, as we familiarised ourselves with our neighbours and the local wildlife, Rose settled into her village school, and I even joined a local CrossFit gym. Life was AMAZING, it was everything I had ever dreamed of. And every time doubts came in about deserving this life, or it all coming crumbling down, I would push them to the back of my mind and tell myself "You have worked hard for this Julie, this is the payoff"

By March though, I was on Prozac, and sleeping most of the day unable to face my new reality, things reached a climax when I ended up having to go to the doctors for emergency tests after thinking I was having a stroke, my blood pressure and cholesterol were at ridiculously high levels (something I had never faced before), as I struggled to come to terms with what was happening.

I had hit rock bottom.

My friends were amazing, my old clients too.

But things were dire.

I had a very small, but incredible support network that carried me through the early few weeks of dealing with this crisis. When I was unable to talk about it publicly.

I was sure I could rebuild, but I also knew that it takes time to launch something new, and time was the one thing I didn't have. My rent was due each month, the credit cards needed paying off, and the cost-of-living increases were hitting me hard for the first time in years.

They say most people are 2 months' salary away from bankruptcy...I'd say I was around 4 months away with my higher costs after moving to the countryside and my gorgeous new home. I had savings, I had assets, I was resourceful... but this redundancy came out of nowhere and it took me a while to accept what was happening and find my feet after the blow.

The hardest thing to accept was that I had left myself so vulnerable in the first place, that my ex-boss knew what this redundancy would have meant for me and my daughter, she had seen me make the big move to the countryside, we had spoken about the increased costs, she hadn't given me a heads up of any kind to help me better protect myself.

I tried to keep things as normal as possible for Rose, but I also made a commitment to myself to try and be honest with what was going on, without scaring her. She needed to know that there was a possibility we might need to move, she needed to know that we would be cutting back on luxuries, and that getting a puppy (the only thing she has ever asked for) was on hold.

Rose has been there every step of my business journey, she celebrates every success, and she has often had to endure my trips overseas, or my long days at work during COVID, before I could go to the park to play... to be fair she's also had trips to Euro Disney and influencer style events to get makeovers as a result of being my daughter... so I think she's had an ok deal overall lol

In April I enrolled Rose into a local Street Dance class, she had been looking for some kind of activity out of school, to help her make friends and to boost her confidence a bit. Things had not been easy for her, moving from the only home she'd ever known, being the only child of colour in our village, one of only a handful of non-white kids at school... a big shift, a big cultural change.

I figured Street dance, in nearby Bishop Stortford, which was more culturally diverse, would be a great choice, and would give me an hour once a week to do the shopping without a child hanging off me.

It might also give me some head space I thought.

When it came to paying the terms fees though, I can remember making the £120 payment from literally the last bit of money I had in my savings account, while she took part in her first paid class after the free trial. I was sat in the foyer of South Mills Arts, and I couldn't stop crying... you know those quiet, discreet tears, you can't keep in.

I felt I had totally let her down in my job as parent.

***I am a fucking failure***

***I have just spent the last £120 in my account on Street dance for Rose***

***I mean how could I tell her "Sorry I can't afford the only thing you enjoy doing" after putting her through this big move so that I could follow my dreams of living in the countryside?***

***I am a fucking liability***

***A burden***

***I can't be trusted***

***I am a useless parent***

***I can't even look after myself, how can I look after a child?***

So yeah, I wasn't exactly in a good frame of mind that day.

How had I let things get to this?

I thought back to all the money I had spent on coaches, and programmes, and tech, and branding, and Virtual Assistants, and flights to conferences, all with the "it will pay off in the future" mindset.

What an idiot I had been.

Why had I not created more safety and security?

All that hype, all that effort, all that energy spent on trying to build a future of abundance, and here I was on the brink of homelessness and financial ruin.

I think it was the first time that I realised how vulnerable I really was as a single mum.

I didn't have parents or a partner to bail me out, and there was only so much my friends could do to support me.

Now, looking back, I can accept that I was only partly responsible for leaving myself so vulnerable. I had done a lot of due diligence when taking on that job, I had sense checked my contract with a whole heap of my peers, but sometimes these things happen. Some people are good at hiding the reality of a situation no matter how hard you look at the risks.

It doesn't have to be redundancy, it could equally have been a health issue, a bereavement, a cyber-attack, or security leak, some bad publicity, a silly investment, a dubious partnership, an abusive relationship... the fact is many of us are always on the edge of vulnerability.

We are back to that chair again

- Financial Security
- Emotional Security
- Spiritual Security
- Physical Security

We need all 4 legs intact... AND we need contingency plans to cover all bases, in case any or all of these break or get worn down, or heaven forbid the environment becomes unsteady for any reason.

Solopreneurship is all fun and games when money is coming through the doors and everything is honky dory in your personal life, but so few of us have the right financial systems in place to

A. Be profitable enough in the first place
B. Ensure we will be Ok if things start to slow down

Far too many Solopreneurs are actually running Loss Leading Businesses without wanting to own up to it.

We have to be the CEO and the CFO too (that's Chief Finance Officer in case you didn't know)

Are you putting money aside for your tax bill?
Are all of your business activities profitable?
Are you leaking money through bad marketing?
Are you paying yourself a fair wage?
Are you planning for emergencies or downturns?

I saw a funny meme while writing this book:

*"If you ever see me talking to myself, just move along, I am self-employed, and we are having a team meeting"*

Funny but actually quite worrying given the increase in mental health challenges amongst this growing demographic, and it is made worse for anyone who is already at a disadvantage or has their head stuck in the sand when it comes to money stuff.

In reality we are the CGO...the Chief Grafting Officer...we do most of the work and have the emotional burden of having to make all the right decisions. It's no wonder we feel exhausted.

We are being bombarded with marketing messages all day every day. How many times do you start the week off with good intentions and before you know it someone else's marketing has taken you off on a tangent....and you are now doing more consuming than producing, more learning than teaching, more deciphering than taking action on the strategy you already agreed on?

There are an estimated 582 million entrepreneurs globally (according to MARKINBLOG 2020) and that surely increased during the pandemic when so many were forced to be resourceful and start up their own ventures.

That's BIG business for people who sell into that market, even if you are in a crowded industry such as business coaching.

Folks are investing a lot of time, money and energy in learning how to influence solopreneurs buying decisions, and the language that is used to hook people in is becoming stronger and stronger.

We start believing that we need things in our business that aren't essential, and for many people doing business online a sale, is a sale, is a sale...they don't care if your business is at the right stage, if you are able to utilise the piece of software you just purchased, or will be able to spend the time needed to do all the things some coaches require you to do to succeed.

THAT'S ON YOU.

Martin Lewis, the founder of the website MoneySavingExpert, is known for his practical and effective advice on personal finance, with a straightforward decision-making process when it comes to buying something.

I think it is equally as powerful for business owners.

1. Can I afford it? Before making a purchase, ask yourself if you can comfortably afford the item without jeopardizing your essential expenses, savings goals, and financial stability. Avoid using credit or loans for non-essential purchases unless you have a solid plan to repay them.
2. Will I use it? Consider whether the item aligns with the actual needs of your business. Will it bring genuine value or utility to your life, or is it likely to become an unused or underutilized resource? Think about the long-term value the item offers.
3. Is it the best deal? If you've determined that the item is necessary and will be used, research to ensure you're getting the best possible deal. Compare prices, look for discounts,

consider buying second hand, and explore various retailers before making your decision.

You know what you want from your business, and you know what you need. Or at least you should do. That is your job as a CEO... don't give away your power to people that know very little about you and your circumstances.

DO NOT GET YOURSELF INTO PERSONAL DEBT TO GROW YOUR BUSINESS.

(Check out my chapter on sales first...sell your way into being able to pay for coaching, equipment or support...you think its chicken and egg, its not... go back to basics and find people who are willing to buy what you have on offer)

Knowing what kind of business you are currently running, AND knowing what kind of business you would like to run, is paramount. Too few solopreneurs even think about this? They are so consumed in the day to day, the next milestone, that they don't think about the bigger picture, or even if they are moving in the right direction.

When I set up my fitness business in 2013 I didn't really think about what kind of business I wanted initially, I just needed it to be profitable and quick, in order to pay my mortgage and cover childcare costs.

A few years in, I realised it was a Legacy business I was growing, a brand that was bigger than me (excuse the pun), but much of the business advice I was getting wasn't fit for purpose... what I needed was a cofounder, or an investor, a team to help me scale it...instead I tried to do it all for too long, and that eventually lead to burnout, and other competitors taking my initial market lead.

There is a lot of talk about scaling in the online world, and it is as a concept often misunderstood among solopreneurs.

Scaling is NOT about making more money through selling more product, scaling is about changing your business model so that you have exponential growth, larger market reach, an expanded product offering; allowing you as the founder to step away from the day to day operations of the business... to the point that you are probably not considered a solopreneur anymore.

And yet we still see Facebook ads targeting one man/woman/person brands with "Are you Ready to Scale Your Business" and they are mainly talking about increasing revenue and being more visible online.

## WHAT KIND OF BUSINESS ARE YOU REALLY RUNNING?

I believe there are 5 types of business

1. Loss Leading
2. Lifestyle
3. Leveraged
4. Liberated
5. Legacy

You can take my FREE business audit to find out which you are running at www.juliecreffield.com/audit

Over 100 small business owners filled this out in the first week I launched it, and more than 90% of them came out as a Loss Leading business, it led to some very interesting conversations.

Most of those loss leading businesses knew they wanted a leveraged or a liberated business, one which they could step away from for extended periods of time, some however knew it was a lifestyle business they wanted... one that was aligned to their values and their specific family set up.

There were literally a small handful that actually wanted a legacy business... even if they didn't quite know how to get there yet... they had big ambitions for sure, even if the roadmap was a bit sketchy.

The truth is there are legacy implications across all 5 of these business types, even if we don't always want to admit it.

The cost of doing business for some people is greater than others, the cost on our health, our self-esteem, our financial security, our relationships, our connection with our kids, our standing in the community.

For some of us we do not have the luxury of time...we can't wait a decade for our businesses to take off.

We do not all have the same opportunities as solopreneurs, just as in life. We make judgements, we have unconscious bias, and there are structures and systems in place that make things easier for some people and harder for others, that is a fact.

I can't compete with a tech savvy 21 year old who has 20 hours a day to work on his venture, no dependants and is living on his friends couch between continents building his luxury digital nomad brand, and neither would I want to.

I can't justify spending huge amounts of money testing paid advertising strategies until I find one that works, shrugging off failure because there are always more opportunities for that big win round the corner.

I can't tap into my parents' little black book, nor their cheque book... neither would get me very far to be fair, and this is often the case for many people who don't come from entrepreneurial or affluent families.

We all have our own set of circumstances that make our way of doing business different, and sometimes that can feel unfair, sometimes it can feel impossible to keep up and compete on an even playing field.

You think you have it bad? There is always someone worse off, always someone with less advantage, less inherent privilege than you. That doesn't make your situation any better, and let's not try and make this a competition for who's the brokest or has the least opportunity... business is challenging in different ways for different people.

We can usually find evidence to the contrary of course, to make ourselves feel better, we can find the folks who "made it" especially when we go look for it, but mostly we live in our own bubbles only ever really seeing things through our own lens... and we rarely see where our own privilege sits when it comes to making money and finding success.

Aside from the challenges of being a neurodiverse, single mum, a woman in business, I have a whole heap of privilege too. I can access spaces others find impossible to navigate safely, I have two decades of project successes behind me, and a massive audience from my previous venture to build upon, I have my health, I have my native language, I have my appearance.

Raphael Sofoluke founder of the UK Black Business Show was sick of the lack of diversity at business events, so he created his own. In his book Twice as Hard he shares the stories of Black Business owners and the lengths they have had to go to before finding success in business, often working twice as hard as their white peers.

In his book he runs through the shocking stats of representation in business settings and the access to funding for black business owners, which informed his decision not to seek external finances for his venture.

He says, *"I did not want to wait on someone else to agree with my dream"*

Similarly, Maddy Alexander-Grout founder of the Mad About Money App has been told time and time again that she needs a cofounder in order to be considered for funding, and she is using her work as a way of showcasing the inequality that still exists for female owned businesses.

The problem is we just don't see the inequality unless it affects us directly... and even then we are told we are imagining it, stop moaning, and just make it work... so we internalise the stress of it being hard, it must be us.

I remember being at a meeting in 2008 on the 22nd floor of the Barclays building in Canary Wharf, I was working for London Councils at the time, Olympic Policy Manager for Volunteering & Community Sport, and around the table were the great and the good from sport and volunteering organisations from around the UK.

We were talking about how we were going to recruit the 70,000 games makers required to service this mega event. One man in his 60s piped up almost immediately as the facilitator opened up the discussions, and he said:

*"Not sure why we need a meeting for this, the UK's sports clubs are headed up by hundreds of experience volunteers who will jump at the chance to support the games... we just need to ask them"*

He was right.

We could have recruited a team of old, white, sports-fanatical men, and probably a bunch of middle-aged white women too, happy to make teas... retirees mainly, folks who love sport, and could probably afford to take 2 weeks of work and come down to London at their own expense.

But would that workforce have really reflected the diversity of London? Would it have been a workforce totally suited to welcoming the 200 nations from all over the world? Would it have been one in keeping with the vibrant, inclusive, forward-thinking brand that London 2012 were working towards?

NOPE.

Another time I saw an invite from Sport England for a breakfast meeting at Lords cricket ground to discuss why women played less sport than men, a meeting about inclusion and equality... and they chose to host the meeting at a time of day where most women who have kids would be unable to attend.

You can't make that shit up.

I see it all the time in the business world, events that always run on a Saturday, events that revolve around alcohol, or venues that are not inclusive for those with a disability, schedules and working practices that are challenging for neurodiverse business owners, speaker line ups that only show a certain demographic and then the organisers wonder why their events don't attract a more diverse audience.

It can be exhausting fighting this stuff when you are also trying to build a business, but being aware of it, calling it out where you can, and being prepared for the fight can help it not beat you.

It can also help you be more decerning with how you spend your money. Who you spend your money with. Shopping local, buying ethical brands, working with smaller companies and individuals, rather than agencies or massive brands that don't give a shit about you...and just make their shareholders richer.

And finally, a word on working for FREE to be helpful, to create good karma, to get access to products or services you can't afford yet in your business. STOP. Most of those arrangements don't work out fair.

People don't value FREE in most situations, it creates a weird set of expectations and conditional energy requirements.

Learn how to make lots of money in your business instead, and pay for services properly...that's how we create a thriving solopreneur economy where we are in control of our business affairs.

I think it's time we had THAT chat about sales... don't you?

## How NOT to be Broke Top Tips

Think about your own set of circumstances, the responsibilities you have to yourself and others, and create a simple set of guidelines for risk and spend in your business.

Get into the habit of assessing need vs want; must-have vs nice to have

Know what kind of business you are REALLY running, take the audit at www.juliecreffield.com/audit I am happy to run through your results with you to see if there any ways of me supporting your growth... most people won't take me up on this, but the offer is there.

Work on your boundaries, practice saying NO, not this time, not for me, when the time is right... without being dragged into thoughts of "not wanting it enough". Your safety and security are paramount.

Encourage win-win situations in business investments, do your due diligence, and look for ways to leverage what you already have to amplify your business before you tap into your reserves.

**Poor (adj.)**

c.1200, "lacking money or resources, destitute of wealth; needy, indigent;" also "small, scanty," also voluntarily and deliberately, "devoid of possessions in conformity with Christian virtues,"

## CHAPTER 7

# *MASTER THE SKILL OF SALES*

***Whether you're selling a product, service, or yourself in a job interview, mastering the art of sales can open doors to numerous opportunities. This skill can bolster your income and offer a backup plan during financial downturns.***

In the world of small business, one truth stands firm: without sales, your venture is merely a hobby... an expensive one at that. I'd go even further and say without profitable sales, your business could quite possibly be considered a charity... doing good in the world, putting in all the hours, but at what expense to you?

While understanding expenses, overheads, and profit margins is important, sales is the engine that brings cash into the business in the first place, allowing it to thrive and grow, and yet it seems to be the thing which solopreneurs resist learning how to do effectively.

Plus, Sales is the thing that saves your bacon when the shit hits the fan.

I remember when COVID hit, and I panicked for around 24 hours and then I sat down and asked myself 3 questions.

1. What do I need to survive

2. What do my clients need
3. What does the world need

This eventually turned into my Triangle of Need model

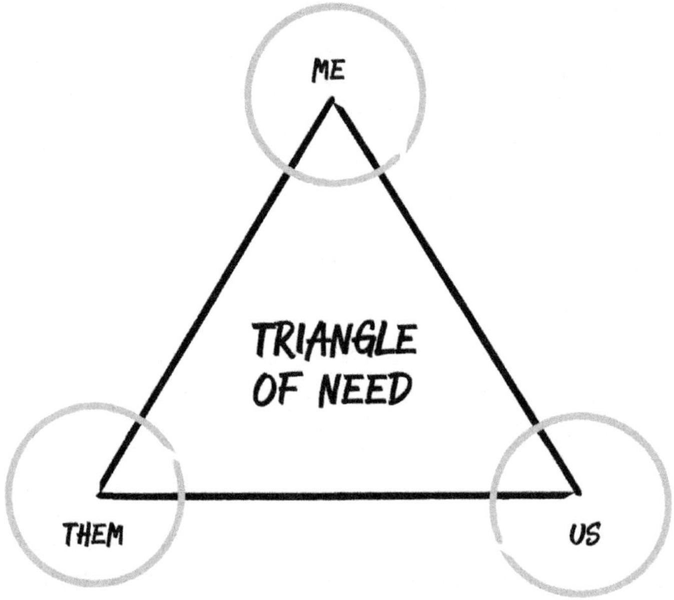


This helped me get out of my head the potential of a financial crash and my ultimate demise, and proved to be insightful whenever I felt stuck on what to offer my audience next to support their challenges.

I didn't want to just survive during the pandemic I wanted to thrive, I had worked too damn hard to get me out of challenging financial situations to let a global bloody pandemic be the death of me.

Sales would be at the heart of this, so I just had to get out of my own way.

I knew I could be of service to business owners who had never had to operate fully online before, I knew I had a good track record of delivering online programmes and products, so I went hell for leather and worked with more than 3000 paying clients that year...each and every one of them needing to go through a sales process of sorts.

Many entrepreneurs find themselves overwhelmed by the prospect of selling, but the truth is, mastering the art, science, and magic of sales is the antidote to financial challenges... and it starts with understanding your emotions around money.

Can you remember how it felt asking your parents for something as a child and they said "NO". Often it wasn't the fact you were not going to get that toy or that bag of sweets, it was the feeling of being rejected, the exchange of value not given, the joy of getting what you want taken away from you.

Rejection sucks... even as an adult.

Then, add to that any conditioning you received growing up around money more generally. Phrases I often heard were...

*"Money doesn't grow on trees"*

*"Want don't get"*

*"It's crass talking about money"*

*"It's not ladylike to be so focussed on money"*

*"Be grateful for what you have got...others are worse off"*

*"Don't rock the boat"*

*"Better safe than sorry"*

I think for women more generally there is a long-standing history of women not considered to be great sales people, or if they are in sales, it is for low cost items, things only women would buy.

Social commentator Selina Todd said "Women did better in positions where they didn't need to compete with men" who still saw women in the workplace and in business as being there to earn "Pin Money".

Just think of all the business models which relied on a female workforce, on women becoming better sales people, Ann Summers, Tuppaware, Zumba...network marketing and the rise of the online influencer, these would have been unimaginable as a route to financial freedom only a few generations ago... but the hangover still exists, and we often hold onto that people pleasing, let's not rock the boat attitude.

Women who do well in sales are often seen as ball breakers or unethical, and so we find ourselves in some kind of no man's land. We must improve this skillset if we want to create real autonomy and freedom in our businesses and lives. It is about valuing what we offer.

Sales isn't just about pushing products or services on people; it's about solving problems, creating value, and building relationships. When you understand this, the sales process becomes less about persuading someone and more about demonstrating how your solution meets their needs.

When it comes to sales and using your business as a vehicle to change your economic situation as a solopreneur, I like to think of money in different ways

1. Launch Income... money which comes in as a direct result of a specific marketing campaign, with beginning and end periods. I have found this the most profitable, but also the most stressful. What is great about launching is you create urgency and containment; you can set targets and measures of success. And once you have a launch system that works you can use this over and over again
2. Evergreen Income... money which comes in across the year from regular marketing, key events and the building of my personal brand. This may be supported by behind-the-scenes infrastructure such as funnels and referrals, but can be a little unpredictable if you don't create some structure around it

3. Passive income... money which comes in without me having to trade my time for money. For me this shows up as book royalties, digital products and affiliate kickbacks for products and services I share. Now, let's not pretend this income is truly passive as there is always some initial work to be done before this kind of income can be unlocked.
4. Unexpected income... some money seems to fall out of the sky, joint ventures, speaking gigs, sponsorship deals, business partnerships, tax rebates, clients needing to work with you to fix an urgent problem.

Each of these have sales and influence at the heart of them.

Someone else, an individual or a company, want something you have and are willing to pay for it. Ultimately, whatever it is you are selling, you need to be totally on top of what the transformation is for the end user, and be relentless in sharing that as widely as possible...even when you think people are not listening, they are.

You have to create a general buzz around you and your business, to allow for some magic to unfold, but equally you must have a process too, a strategy.

What I often see with business owners is a lack of understanding of what it takes to create sales, enough sales to get you firmly out of the feast and famine cycle, enough sales to have a viable sustainable business.

Too many solopreneurs subscribe to the "build it and they will come" motto, and the truth is: if there are other people selling what you have to offer, then they have choice, they may have an abundance of choice, and then it becomes your job to cut through the noise and to convince folks that buying from you is the best option.

But I hate that energy of having to convince people to pick you, don't you?

This is where building your personal brand, and becoming what Daniel Priestly calls a Key Person of Influence is important, building what Seth Godin calls a *Tribe* around you and your business.

One of the reasons that my fitness business was so successful is that I was first to market in the UK with a plus size fitness running brand, one that was 100% online. I was a Key Person of Influence, the go to person for brands and end users.

I had an online community of more than 50K plus size women cheering me on, wanting to be active customers, wanting to help me grow the brand. AND I had regular PR and engagement opportunities through brand partnerships, races and speaking gigs to keep me front of mind for my people.

But after around 3 or 4 years of being in business, other plus size fitness folks started to emerge, in fact I remember appearing on a podcast with Martinus Evans, founder of 300lbs and Running... who has built a fitness empire in the US based on my business model.

The market had changed, people were still buying but not as many, they now had more choice. It wasn't as unique. By the time the pandemic came, EVERYONE was offering online fitness programmes and classes, and inclusion was the buzz word.

I had missed my opportunity to scale.

But I knew how to sell, I had an engaged audience, so I just had to evolve my offer.

Making sales in your business always starts with working out what it is you want. When I ask clients how much they want to make in this launch, they often reply:

*"I need to make £3000 to cover my bills"*

Which always makes me laugh.

*"YES, but how much do you WANT to make?"*

It comes down to desire... and whether you are driven by away-from goals or towards goals.

An away-from sales goal might be something like, *"I need to sell 4 coaching programmes before the end of this month otherwise I can't pay my outstanding tax bill, and I might have to go and get a "proper" job"*

A towards sales goal might be something like *"I would like to make £10,000 or more from this launch, I'd like to have enough money in the bank to cover my expenditure for the next couple of months, AND to treat myself and my family to a mini break"*

How you think about your sales goals matters.
Having clear sales targets matters.
Reviewing your sales tactics matters.

When you know what you want, we can then build a sales strategy around that. If we are always coming from a place of need, a place of "just enough" then we are always playing catch up and there is very little wriggle room if the sales process doesn't work out.

Some of this is about pricing.

Do you want to sell 100 x £100 product or service

Or 2 at £5000

What feels easier, what feels more in alignment with your values, your business brand, where your ideal client is right now.

Too many solopreneurs just don't have a strategy when it comes to sales, they (you guessed it) use hope as a strategy, and then get disappointed when growing their business feels like a slog.

I was there too. It took me years to finally accept that crossing my fingers and shouting about my offers a few times would not be enough...it wasn't, it never is... not in the long term anyway.

I like to keep things simple.

If I want to make £10,000 there are various ways I can make it

- £10,000 payment
- 2 x £5000
- 10 x £1000
- 20 x £500
- 50 x £200
- 100 x £100
- 200 x £50
- 1000 x 10

And, of course, other variations.

Do you know how many of your products and services you need to make to hit your sales targets, by launch or across the year?

Are you able to say X number of sales this year = an X figure business, or X amount of profit?

Once you know what you want, you then have to look at some other important numbers

- How many people you have on your email list
- How many fans you have on social media (very hard to measure btw)
- How many people do you have in your wider networks
- How many communities of your ideal clients you can infiltrate
- How big the market is for what you are offering, and do you have a route to that market for example speaking at a high-profile event or paying for Facebook adverts?

It is a numbers game.

Wanting to sell 100 places on a £500 programme, when you only have 30 people on your email list, no funds for paid advertising and a fear of visibility makes hitting that target difficult, not impossible but improbable.

It is always a numbers game, and yet so many of us are afraid to even look at the numbers

- Conversion Rates: How many leads turn into paying customers?
- Customer Acquisition Cost: How much are you spending to get one new customer?
- Lifetime Value: Over time, how much is each customer worth to your business?

Understanding these metrics helps you focus on what's working and adjust what isn't.

Simply saying *"I am just no good at sales"* isn't enough of an excuse... get good.

I think this starts with being OK with a no.

A lot of sales trainers teach to deal with objections, to think about the reasons people are likely to use to say no, and to address those, so people simply can't say NO... I call bullshit on that tactic.

I want people to be OK with saying NO.

I love being confidently pitched, as long as folks are OK with me saying NO.

If you have a good enough lead generation system you don't need EVERYONE to buy form you anyway, and often a NO becomes a NOT YET, and often a NO leads to a positive conversation about why not, which unlocks further insight into your ideal client.

If we listened more when folks told us no, when we believe they are an ideal client and "should" buy, but they don't, we would be able to improve our products and services, and our marketing, and ultimately improve our business.

Often, we don't have enough data to use in that assessment process.

When I am in a launch, I expect to have hundreds of conversations with people, most of whom won't buy. The more conversations I have the more sales I make though, so I just need to encourage people to talk to me, to share with me their problems and their goals.

I also understand the energetic cost of being in sales mode... coping with heightened emotions and managing expectations, and whatever the eventual outcome of the sales push is (good or bad, there will be an effect).

Building in self-care during times of high sales activity is crucial... and not letting the outcome, good or bad, define you.

Having a process which you feel comfortable with really helps, because then you can take some of the emotion out of it and just follow the process.

I call mine the Grand in Your Hand Process... based on the premise that at any given time I can go to my audience and make £1000 at will...and I believe you can to.

Do that enough, and you have a business that generates £10,000 per month, £100K a year, £1 million even...the numbers are irrelevant, it all comes down to what it is you want, and being able to communicate that to enough of your ideal audience.

It can be done from a standing start, but can also be layered, launch upon launch, so that you have some momentum going into it.

Oh, and repetition.

We must get comfortable with sounding like a broken record lol

We do love to mess with a system even when it working; a lot of sales is about following the system and repeating yourself, over and over again.

Think about your favourite brands and how they do sales... it is often rinse and repeat right?

OK so here is my Grand in Your Hand sales process.

This can be done over 10 days or 10 hours... anything longer than that and the strategy needs a bit of tweaking, anything short of that, and folks don't get the full effect.

1. Get clear on how much you want to make, and why... share this with a business buddy or loved one for extra accountability, post the amount somewhere you can see it clearly
2. Get clear on what it is you are selling. Not the product or the service, but the transformation. Think about what's going on in the world NOW, and if your current products and services are the right fit for this. You can sell something new, or something old (just packaged differently). Make your offer as compelling as possible... a total no brainer for people to say yes to
3. Do the maths... be super clear on how many of these products and services you need to hit your target. Create a good, great, and amazing target. Commit to finding those sales, but also be open to money coming in via other streams... increased visibility often leads to other things flying off the shelves.
4. Get folks to put their hands up... you want people to tell you that they need your services, on social media this is easy (it's called engagement), in person at an event you can simply ask "who has this problem". This is selling with consent. You don't have to tell them what the product or service is, or how much it costs or when it starts, you just want to create intrigue, curiosity and some social proof/excitement around your launch... this would be a good point to start a Prospect List

# THE HANDS UP PROCESS

1. Make it easy... go to your low hanging fruit first. Do some covert sales either with hot prospects, or closed communities. Incentivise some early adopters, so that when you start to talk more publicly you can share that 25% of the availability has already been snapped up... we call this scarcity.
2. Let's talk impact... sometimes selling is simply sharing stories of transformation and asking who else would like to come and play... share case studies and testimonials, share what the product or service does.
3. Social proof... celebrate each and every sale as it comes through, people like to know that it is safe to buy, and if others are doing it, then maybe they could too.
4. Have an end date... have a closing date for this offer, and as you get closer to this time, reach out to those on your prospect list, have as many converting conversations as you can, and share what comes up from them (confidentially of course)

there will be folks on the fence deciding whether to buy, they might just need some prompting.

5. Mopping up... there are always some last-minute stragglers. Check on where people are. Push for a no, or a not this time, start a prospect list for your next launch. Start looking at your numbers.
6. Celebration time... acknowledge not only the outcome but the output, celebrate publicly if you feel comfortable, how excited you are to be doing the work, what you intend to spend the money on...let folks who didn't buy know you still love and respect them, and that there is always next time.

It is normally around the closing time that there is the most interest in your work...the peak of activity, and yet often in the launch period, many solopreneurs give up long before then, meaning folks haven't had long enough to consider your offer... or they haven't been reminded enough to take action.

If a launch "doesn't work" the first time round, it may next time... it may with a different offer, a down sell towards the end maybe?

The biggest breakthroughs in my sales challenges which teach this method are not always from the clients who make the most money, they are from the ones who don't hit their targets, because we explore why, and that unlocks either a mindset issue or a structural business issue which needs addressing.

The thing which folks report back to me as one of the biggest wins from the challenge are allowing yourself to "fail", to set big targets and to miss them, knowing it's not the end of the world.

I have had clients make their first $20 of passive income, right up to £27,000 in consultancy fees by taking part... and business owners come back time and time again for a little bit more sales activation and magic.

FEAR is what holds us back from selling

The fear of failure AND the fear of success. Who would I be if I hit all my targets? Who would I be if I was super successful? Who would I be without the stress and drama of not having enough?

A client I have been working with for many years told me,

*"I'd have to wear white linen trousers if I made £50K a month, because that's what wealthy women wear right?"*

We laugh about it now, but that comment illustrates just how weird and whacky our money blocks can be.

My biggest tip for overcoming the fear of selling is to look at it as an adventure, an experiment, to explore each part of your sales process with a sense of wonder, a sense of curiosity.

I wonder if I could... xyz?
What if I managed to... xyz?
Where might I be able to... xyz?
How can I find... xyz?

It is all about learning what works for your business, for your audience, for your personality and style, and building your sales capabilities.

It is also about unpacking the negative emotion that comes with not hitting your targets, not even setting targets. Keeping ourselves emotionally safe. Playing small. Staying within our comfort zones.

I consider myself extremely lucky that as part of my training in the arts in the early part of my career, I learned to die. PUBLICLY. Improvisation played a huge part of my degree course, and I also did a few additional projects around stand-up comedy. Even now as a professional keynote speaker there will be moments where your mind goes blank, or a story doesn't resonate with your audience.

The truth is some jokes die a death

Sometimes, when trying something new, it flops
You have to learn to not have it define you, and to lean more into what does work
Never letting go of the magic of experimentation

Understanding sales is not just a means to prevent your business from going broke; it's the lifeline that will allow it to flourish.

By shifting your mindset to view sales as a value-driven process, investing in skills development, and leveraging metrics and networks, you position your small business for financial success and stability.

Remember, every thriving business is built on a foundation of consistent and effective sales efforts, but from time to time your finances can shift significantly without much warning. Yes, in hindsight, we'd all like to have a rainy day fund, or assets we can unlock, but the truth is many of us just don't.

Learning how to sell ANYTHING but especially YOU will be the thing which saves you.

### How NOT to be Broke Top Tip

Come and take part in my **How NOT to be Broke Sales challenge**, I run it live 3 times a year, but you can buy it to work through the process by yourself at any point... and it gives you a pass to join live at any point.

The sooner you register, the cheaper it always is too... fortune favours the fast lol

Find out more at www.juliecreffield.com/broke

Want a mini challenge to get you started? Whatever it is you are selling right now, find 100 ideal clients and go and talk to them. Build rapport and then ask for the sale. Try to do this in a day or a week for the sense of urgency. Make notes on what works, the success rate, what feedback you get... and, most importantly, how you feel.

**Rich (adj.)**

Old English rice "strong, powerful; great, mighty; of high rank" Old English. Old English also had a noun, *rice* "rule, reign, power, might; authority; empire" The meaning "magnificent" is from c. 1200; that of "of great value or worth" is from mid-13c. The evolution of the word reflects a connection between wealth and power in the ancient world, though the "power" sense seems to be the oldest.

## CHAPTER 8

# *DIVERSIFY AND CONQUER*

***Relying on a single income stream or investment is a risky game. The more diverse your sources of income and investments, the better protected you are from financial downturns, and the more flexible you can be in acquiring wealth.***

Just as nature thrives on diversity, so your financial portfolio should thrive on a mix of assets. By spreading your resources across various opportunities, you reduce the risk of total loss and increase the potential for growth.

But where to start? And what do you do if you feel you have left it too late?

When you are in typical feast and famine mode as a solopreneur, or when you have any kind of insecurity or instability going on, it is difficult to make a commitment to long term savings and investments.

This is amplified if you have to research the ins and outs of any potential investments, whether that be developing a new business offering or starting in crypto currency... don't worry I am not going anywhere near that in this book.

Nobody ever told me about investing for my future. I mean that was something I would think about when I grew up... and at 45 I am only just realising that this is NOW. It's astonishing where time goes, and the impact of putting off some of these important financial decisions. I am not beating myself up about it, I am instead choosing to make a start now.

Should I have learned some of this stuff earlier? YES, but to be fair I have read many books over the years, watched many masterclasses and even invested in an "investing for idiots" style programme... but my ADHD brain struggles with a lot of this, and it all feels a little risky.

Plus, for a decade I have been raising another human being single headedly, leaving me responsible for all day-to-day costs, and trust me having a fashion crazy, boba drinking, mini me... who I have taught to enjoy the finer things, that hasn't always been cheap or easy.

Whenever I have had the capacity, either financial or mindset-wise, I have found myself spiralling and not being able to decide on the right approach. My ADHD probably comes into full force here too.

This is where financial literacy, not through books, but through having real long-term mentors can work in your favour. I have a bit of a mistrust of financial advisors, mainly because I don't know how it all works, what the structures are that drive that profession, i.e. will they look after my money as well as I will (or won't lol)

The first I ever thought about pensions for example was when I got my first local authority job in my mid-twenties and I had to opt out of the pension scheme rather than opt in, my Aunt who worked for the same local council as a nursery nurse said "Oh stay in the pension... it's a good one" so I did.

I managed 8 years of continuous service over all and now have a small pension to look forward to, and a tidy little death grant for Rose which she can enjoy whenever I pop my clogs... I regret not further investing in a pension, the timing never seemed right though, and the shame I have around that decision still lingers.

I am committed to exploring this now though, maybe it isn't too late.

I do have life insurance and I also have an apartment in East London, so it's not like I haven't made any sensible long term money decisions over the years, but possibly not enough and in many ways I have been relying on hope as a strategy, believing that all it would take would be one best-selling book and I could live off the royalties for life.

If I sell a million copies of How NOT to be Broke, maybe I will be OK after all hey?

Oh, and a few years ago I started to invest in Gold Bullion... that feels pretty abundant, and low risk in many ways... I have this image of one day needing to flee war or the effects of global warming, and taking my gold bullion to use as payment for some kind of safe passage lol

But anyway, those are my tangible assets.

Probably not a lot to show for a lifetime of hard graft... compared to some.

I often wonder if some of my poor financial decision-making has been a result of having an absence of financially savvy caregivers in my life. My Dad left when I was 12 and was shocking with money, and my Mum was a typical bury your head in the sand kinda person when it came to money, to which she is kind of paying the price for now in retirement.

I have not had a life partner to discuss some of these things with either, or to make joint investments. The investing legend Warren Buffest says:

*"The biggest decision of your life will be who you choose to marry"*

He says there have been *"two turning points in my life, one when I came out of the womb and one when I met Susie,"* Buffett says of his first wife, who died in 2004. *"What happened with me would not have happened without her."*

Researchers from Carnegie Mellon University agree that your choice of life partner is totally linked to your success. They brought 163 married couples into the lab and gave one member of each couple a choice: either solve a simple puzzle, or take the opportunity to compete for a prize. The researchers then recorded the couples' interactions as they decided whether to take on the challenge.

Participants with more encouraging partners were substantially more likely to decide to compete for the prize, while those with partners who discouraged them or expressed a lack of confidence more often chose the simple puzzle.

I have been single most of my adult life... not something I am proud of, but also not something I am ashamed of. There is both a single person tax, and a single parent tax...which have cost me greatly over the years... that's before we talk about the gender pay gap.

It is easy to fall into a black hole of regret, and comparison, in years past we didn't really worry about such things, the people who lived down our roads pretty much earned the same as us, our aspirations were similar... but with TV, movies, and of course social media it is easy to get whooped up into a frensy of consumerism and feeling like everyone else is richer than you.

Building wealth shouldn't be about comparing yourself to others. It should be about creating safety, security and freedom, based on your specific values and aspirations, and on your terms.

And yet, there are a lot of online influencers and investment opportunities... also known as get-rich-quick schemes, which pick at these painful wounds, and contribute to your sense of urgency about finally sorting this stuff out.

But while we are figuring out how to become millionaires, we are missing out on the opportunity to use small incremental contributions to our wealth, that over time compound, and create a more sustainable approach to wealth creation.

I remember saving for the deposit of my home.

I was working full time for a local authority, paying into the pension scheme, and there wasn't a lot left over. My boyfriend at the time was a nice guy, but we were living on the 9$^{th}$ floor of a tower block in Hackney and he had no desire to own property... I had no desire to raise a family in a tower block... so eventually we parted ways, but not before I had started to amass some savings. Possibly to buy a home, possibly to pay for rent, either way as a safety net.

I took on some extra freelance work, a couple of nights a week, with some annual leave and occasionally on a Saturdays working on a youth arts programme in Southend. The day rate was good, and it felt like bonus money... money I could easily stash away.

I started saving £150 per month, and it didn't take long before I got the bug for saving, seeing the amount increase over a 12-month period. Before I knew it, I had £15,000, enough for the deposit for a part buy part rent property which was all the rage back then...and probably the only way I would have got on the property ladder as a single person in London.

The other thing I did was I applied for a new job. I knew my £26K a year job wouldn't give me the mortgage amount I needed, and so despite loving my job working with local volunteers in the lead up to the London 2012 games... I started looking for higher paid full time work.

I applied for a £100K job, heading up volunteering policy for a national charity.

I still can't believe I did that. I didn't even get an interview as I was clearly lacking experience and gravitas at this early stage of my career, but I always think "they might have been having an off day" it set me on the right path, of thinking anything was possible.

And a few months later I was successful in securing an ideal next job for me, Olympic Policy Manager for Volunteering & Sport at London Councils, a regional local authority body, that looked after the 33 boroughs in London... the salary was £36K... and that jump enabled me to secure my first home.

I lived in that property for 16 years; it gave me the safety and security that I craved growing up. Even when I was made redundant after becoming a homeowner, the drive to keep up my mortgage payments and to not become homeless was very much informed by the identity I loved... that of being a homeowner.

Small and steady most definitely wins the race, when acquiring assets, building foundations.

It is the same in business.

You start off with nothing but a seed of an idea and then over time you create everything you need to have a thriving business, but it is near on impossible to do it all at once, unless you have unlimited resources and a clear strategy.

Imagine if you were able to take £150 or £1500 or £15,000 out of your business every month to invest or reinvest into something which pays dividends later down the line, but without impacting on your current safety and security?

15 years into the world of online business and I have websites, and funnels, and email automation systems, I have 14 books, I have digital products, I have services and consulting offers. I have thousands and thousands of articles, and press mentions, I have an audience of over 100,000 followers, all things I was able to leverage when life got tough...

The question I often hear from new clients is:

*"What should I start on first?"*

Business owners, even those starting out, know they want many of these things I list above for their own business, but you can't do all of it all at one time, and so I often refer them to Masloes hierarchy of needs, to better understand the urgency of growing their business.

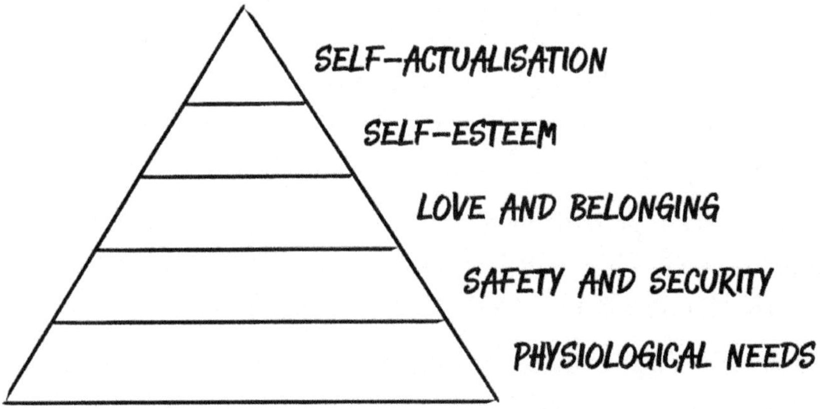


It gets us talking about the specifics of that persons situation, and helps us have an interesting conversation around the difference between push and pull goals, and creating safety and security as a priority.

My strategic advice as a business coach isn't a one size fits all. The advice I would give to a solopreneur who is responsible for 100% of the households living costs, would be totally different to someone who's business is more an outlet for their passion, and there is no pressure to make money from it immediately.

I do always ask what the end goal is though.
What's the point?
Where are you trying to get to?
What's the mission?
What world problem (big world or your world) are you trying to solve?

A lot of solopreneurs get stuck here because they just don't know (and that's OK), but you must keep asking yourself these questions, otherwise you may end up taking your business, and therefore your life, in a direction that isn't fit for purpose.

I did a lot of work over my 8 years working on the London 2012 on the Legacy Masterplan, a 25-year plan to maximise the investment and the experience of the Olympic & Paralympic Games.

I worked with politicians, city planners, community groups, young people... those it would ultimately effect in the lead up to the games, and far beyond.

Imagine if that plan didn't exist.
Imagine if the architects, the town planners, the event organisers, just decided to wing it... to see how it all unfolds?

Imagine if they didn't consult with the stakeholders that it would impact... and just did what they wanted to do, with no input or consideration?

Imagine if they missed the big milestone moments?

You don't need a 25-year plan, but knowing where you are likely to be in 25 years and understanding how your needs might have changed across that time period is pretty important, as is making sure your plan works for those affected by it most.

This is the work I do with my Legacy Masterplan Incubator clients... they are established solopreneurs, often with more than 20 years' experience behind them. They have done all the experiments, they have ridden the waves of adventure... but it is now about consolidation, and being intentional about the time they have left on this planet, and the impact they want to have from their life's work.

It's BIG stuff, right?

But even on a different level, we all need a route map... even if it is to get us to the end of this year in one piece? How can we know what to focus on each day if we don't know the direction of travel or what we are even trying to achieve?

One of the first things I did when the pandemic hit was to create a 1 page "Thrive or Survive" business strategy template for my clients and followers, I offered it for FREE and I delivered a number of workshops around it, to help folks through the fear and uncertainty.

60 minutes of thinking this through meant these business owners now had a plan, they had some options, they had hope YES, but not as a strategy... instead as fuel to keep the strategy (which they now had on a 1 page print out) to keep them focussed and in momentum.

My clients who stayed connected to that plan, that vision for success despite the challenging environment, well let's just say they did some amazing things, and came out of the pandemic stronger for the adversity that it provided us all with.

I help solopreneurs with this via my Solopreneur Success Roadmap programme, we build out a 5-year strategic plan, create a 12-month activation plan, and then we get cracking on making shit happen.

We work on:

1. Clarity... what it is you do and why
2. Confidence... the model, what you sell, how and in what volumes

3. And attracting enough of the right Clients... with ease and into a big enough market

All of which come as a result of having a plan, and actioning it in a consistent, uplifting and creative way, with support and encouragement through the scary bits... and of course keeping an eye on the metrics that matter.

We live in fast moving times, especially in business. The economy is constantly evolving. The more technical automation comes in, the more we will need to rely on our intuition and creativity to find our place in the world.

We cannot be driven by fear, we cannot wait for things to improve, we cannot use hope as a strategy.

What we must do is take steps, big and small, towards the things that we want... and if we do that enough, we create assets that can be leveraged when the shit hits the fan, we can dial up our business activities when we need them, and wind them down when that makes sense too.

I mean isn't that the flexibility that we came into entrepreneurship for?

Or did we just want to make a really difficult job for ourselves, with bad pay, bad working conditions, and no hope for ever retiring.

In the next chapter you will find out how I structure my time to ensure I am always diversifying and building upon my asset base as a serial entrepreneur, but also how I ensure I am living in the present and not putting off life stuff...like dating, and spending time with loved ones.

We can have it all... we just can't do it all... not all at once.

So, we must get focussed on what is possible, and pick a lane.

When you know where it is you want to go with your business... you then need to start building the ship and encouraging people to get onboard.

I use a very simple way of brainstorming products and services, which I call Rocket to the Stars... or let's put a rocket up your arse, depending on the urgency.

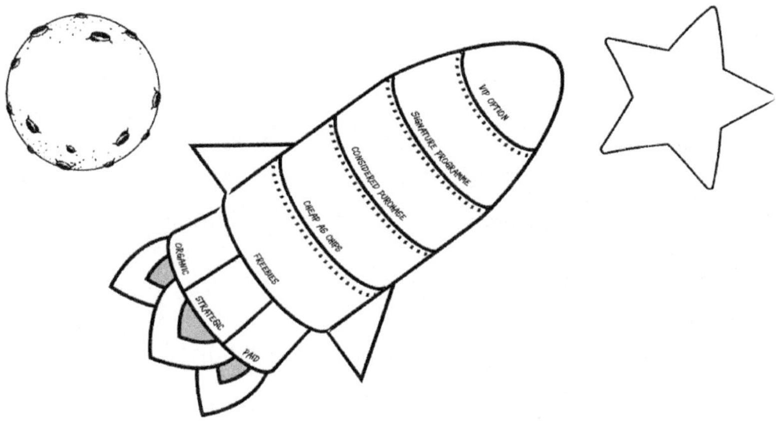


It ALWAYS starts with where you want to get to.

YES, there are other metrics that matter, but I use income as my guiding star. I pick a number and I put that in my star box, I make it a stretch goal, something that feels exciting and juicy... no one wants to slog it out all year for a mediocre target.

I then put in a second number... more of a "must make" number in the moon box. This reminds me that I have to be profitable, I am not in this for the shits and giggles... if I don't hit that target, something is wrong... I may need to re-strategize.

So, whether my rocket reached the moon or the stars, it's all good. You win... or you learn....the longer you stay hitting your moon numbers and never getting into the stars, the more bumpy the ride is likely to be. FACT.

One of my favourite quotes as a child was:

*"Aim for the stars, you might not get there but you will get further than if you just aim for the moon"*

Starting with the money sets the intention, its starts with the WHY and the WHO, before we get on to the WHAT and the HOW... Why is making this money important and who do you need to be to have a business like that?

Then we move on to the fuel.

Something has to get this rocket off the ground, and that something is ALWAYS people. You will need to find clients, collaborators and cheerleaders...and that means building an audience.

You can do this

- Organically... through social media, speaking, and networking
- Via Strategic Partnerships... joint ventures, collaborations, PR
- Paid Advertising... Social media adverts, paid media

My suggestion would be to do a combination of all 3, but don't stretch yourself too thin. Pick some simple but effective audience building systems, ALWAYS with a view to getting folks on your email list... the only true audience container that you own and control is your email list... DO NOT PUT THIS OFF.

When my life fell apart in the Spring of 2023, I didn't have the heart to show up on social media, to admit that my new exciting job hadn't worked out, and to activate my online audience...that felt too scary.

I didn't have anything to offer my strategic partners, and paid advertising was off the table as I had no money to invest at that point.

So, I had to rely on my list... to get me back on my feet again. My list and my close network of business buddies who were an absolute lifeline.

I have been building my email list for 8 years, I have for the past few years had around 5000 subscribers (so not huge... but mainly superfans and current clients), with folks coming and going all the time. It is pretty well segmented, in that I can choose to send emails to small groups based on what programmes they have already done with me.

I sent 3 emails.

1. To my friends, peers, and closest clients (around 30 individuals)
2. To my super fans (folks who had been in my world for more than 5 years who had bought multiple products from me... probably around 1500)
3. To my whole list

The first email was a surrender email, a "hands up my life has just gone to shit" kind of email. It was to address and release the shame I had around the business partnership failing, and it was a genuine ask for help.

The second email was similar but less emotive, and it was my thoughts on what I would do next, to test the market, to see if anyone would like to come with me on that journey. It was the drawing of a line in the sand, a decision around coming to my own rescue.

The third, I only sent once I was confident I had a plan, and it was absolutely the start of a sales email sequence to activate my audience to buy from me again, to invest in my new brand The Year to Change®

Those 3 emails generated around £10,000 in revenue over a 3-week period.... money that allowed me to keep my head above water after not being paid for 3 months.

The following 10-20 emails generated around £30,000 of revenue, alongside some basic social media content, and regular-ish blogging and speaking efforts. This was a combination of some 1-2-1 business coaching, a beta round of a new life coaching programme, and a low-cost digital product.

This makes it sound super simple. It was not. Emotionally it felt really hard. But I also had to remind myself that much of this was customer loyalty that I had built over the years. My audience was a valuable asset, my ability to use new ideas, new concepts, to activate my audience was an asset, my absolute necessity to bring in income and QUICK, well that was an asset... the power of being broke can in fact create miracles.

It was only when my confidence returned that I went back to emailing my list weekly, and being more active on social media, and lining up PR opportunities and partnerships... my email list is what saved me.

For many years I have taught solopreneurs how to grow engaged audiences to support their business, social media might feel like where you build success, but it is 100% the email list where all the fun stuff happens.

Too many solopreneurs put this off. They feel like they don't have enough to say, they don't feel like they have enough time to write content, they don't feel like they could cope with the rejection of people unsubscribing.

A client told me,:

*"You send a LOT of emails, but I look forward to them, I read them all, I miss them when they don't arrive"* she has spent around £2000 with me over the last couple of years.

Another client told me:

*"Being on your email list is like being in a really juicy soap opera, I tune in to see what you are up to... I don't want to miss anything"*

He is a great referral partner, and he engages on LinkedIn with my social posts a lot, bringing me new clients.

GET YOUR EMAIL LIST UP AND RUNNING ASAP

If you already have one, email them today and remind them who you are, how you can help them, and make an offer...see what magic happens.

Right.

So, we now have your direction of travel, and we have the fuel that is going to help you blast off... now we need to build out the actual rocket, the vehicle that will help you achieve your business goals.

This is where you plan out your products and services. This is sometimes known in the industry as your product ladder... your funnel, a way of guiding people into your world with a range of entry points.

Watertight marketing founder Bryony Thomas gets infuriated by the idea of a funnel.

*"Most businesses don't have a funnel they have something more akin to a colander, with leads and customers leaking out all over the place"*

Great marketing, a clear brand, and amazing customer experience will ensure those leaks become smaller and smaller, oh, and AMAZING products and services, that do what they say they do and more.

If you want to have a flexible business with diversification built in, then you want to be able to have a range of price points so that most people can give you money... this is not the same as working with everyone, not everyone will be able to afford all of your stuff, and that's OK.

There are 5 levels to your rocket:

1. **Freebie...** ways to give value and encourage people to engage, and ultimately join your email list. This could be a regular high value blog, it could be lead magnets, it could be events and masterclasses. This is where many of your paying clients will start to engage with you... but not all.
2. **Cheap as chips...** entry level paid products, some people won't need a freebie and they will come straight in and pay for your stuff. This could be a book, a £7 download, a £19 mini product, a ticket to your event, a branded t-shirt. There are some rules with cheap as chips: you must celebrate your new customer make them feel valued... but they cannot get any live time with you; it cannot cost you more to serve them than the small amount of money they are paying; you must be able to sell these things at volume with ease.
3. **A Considered Purchase...** this is a mid-priced product that folks may have to stop and consider A. Whether they need it right now, and B/ if they are going to get a return on their investment. They may get some access to you, but we are still talking multiple people buying this product without it causing you additional work. This could be a membership, events, an online programme, a more detailed digital product, and maybe (if you have capacity) pour hours, or small blocks of access to you.
4. **Signature Programme...** this is where you want all roads leading to, it is your MAIN OFFERING, the thing you are known for, the thing that people refer you for, the thing you are likely to have a wait list for, people making a note to invest with you at some point. For me, when you have clarity on this, the other things seem to sell themselves.

5. **VIP Option...** and this is where the fun stuff happens, when folks are willing to pay a premium to get close to you and your expertise. VIP strategy days, retreats, having folks on a retainer, done-for-you work.... all the bells and the whistles.

Now before you get overwhelmed.

You do NOT need to have all of these in place. But having at least 3 of these in place gives you a better chance of being able to activate your audience.

There is a lot of bullshit out there about what people want: high ticket, low ticket, high volume, premium services... you get to decide which you want to offer, your audience however, decide what they are willing to pay.

I have seen folks who are adamant that they will only sell high ticket due to the transformation they give their clients... and they sit there broke, with NO CLIENTS, when their competitors are out there serving their audience at a range of price points and building client loyalty and market reach.

The truth is the market is always changing, your competitors are out there trying new things, changing up their offers, piloting new things... and you must do this too.

There is a school of thought around picking a niche and creating a signature programme and sticking to it...but I think:

A. That is a bit old school thinking
B. It stinks of privilege

Often the people saying this already have a big following and are known for one thing... even if they have done many things over their career. They may have been first to market with a concept like Seth Godin and Tribes.

But I think this can keep you stuck, it can keep you thinking you have to stick with a sinking ship, it keeps you thinking there is no point, because someone else got their first.

My signature programme for example used to be a programme called Tribe Builder.

When I came up with the idea, I almost talked myself out of it because Seth Godin was the one known for that... but I had been obsessed with community, and tribes since my early career, in fact my degree research was on exactly this area, and my Masters explored online community... long before Facebook groups were even a thing.

I loved that programme.

I ran 6 rounds of it, and helped more than 200 solopreneurs build movements that matter.

My client Heather, launched 1 million women walking, another client launched a campaign called I AM ADHD, another We Are The Unheard... mission led campaigns and projects to drive business, and increase the reach of their work.

However, post pandemic the calls for white influencers and coaches to stop using the word Tribe become louder, and I realised I didn't feel aligned with it anymore, despite initially arguing that my work was different.

And so I moved more into Audience Activation, and the need for Strategic Road Mapping for business owners.

I now have two signature programmes:

- The Solopreneur Success Roadmap... AKA The Roadmap
- The Legacy Masterplan

Which serve slightly different audiences.

Our businesses evolve, they have to. We must learn to be flexible and fluid. For sure we can build successful solopreneur businesses doing one thing, running the same programmes, selling the same products for years and years.

But what if that market dries up?

Look what happened during the pandemic? I saw so many of my speaker buddies' businesses fall off a cliff in an instant, and they were forced to diversify. In fact, I helped many of them take their offline expert-based businesses, into viable online businesses serving the same and new audiences, just in a different way... and I helped them do this fast, before they ran out of reserves and hope.

We live in fast moving times. The economy is constantly evolving. The more technical automation comes in the more we will need to rely on our intuition and creativity to find our place in the world.

We will survive in this new world by learning to live intuitively and going with the flow, there is no going back, we either get with the new technology or we get taken over. We will have to educate ourselves and become an expert in a niche (where tech can't compete), we have to be of service.

We must learn to invest in the future, and for that to happen, we have to free up and create excess resource NOW... by any means necessary.

### How NOT to be Broke Top Tip

Create a financial investing plan and give yourself 6 months to try it out. Switch out something you are willing to sacrifice, an amount that you don't mind losing (you won't miss) and see how you get on.

Invest in building your email list. Make today your day 1 if you haven't nailed this yet... you will thank yourself for this in 6 months. Get on my list www.juliecreffield.com/broke but we warned I communicate with my people A LOT... I want them to remember who I am, I want to share my thoughts on how to be successful.

Think about how you can creatively generate income to invest in specific projects. Set yourself some investing rules. For example, here are a few of mine...

- I will sell 3 discounted 121 power hours with me each month, and use this revenue to invest in paid advertising without worrying about the ROI
- I will use all book royalties to invest in stocks and shares, or gold bullion
- I will take 10% of all speaking gig revenue and put that in my "exciting events/conferences to attend" savings pot
- I will invest/donate 5% of all annual profits to my chosen charity StreetChild

**Business (n.)**

Old English *bisignes* (Northumbrian) "care, anxiety, occupation," from *bisig* "careful, anxious, busy, occupied, diligent" (see **busy** (adj.)) + **-ness** The original sense is obsolete, as is the Middle English sense of "state of being much occupied or engaged" (mid-14c.). The modern two-syllable pronunciation is from 17c.

CHAPTER 9

# *TIME IS PRECIOUS*

***Understand that while money can be earned back, time cannot. Value your time. Spend it wisely, grab those short term wins often, but also invest in long-term growth, and ensure you are giving time to both professional and personal growth.***

And if things need to change, like REALLY change...

Give yourself a year!

Do you ever wish you could have a remote control to go back in time to erase your mistakes or return to easier, simpler times gone past? Or perhaps you'd simply like to press pause and enjoy the time you are in now, without the pressure of having to make big moves in order to have that brighter future.

When I was a kid, I couldn't wait for time to move forward, I was always hoping for brighter days, wishing myself older so I could have more autonomy and freedom, curious to see what adulthood would look like. Now of course at 45, I am like, where on earth has all that time gone.

The truth is we can't control time, often we struggle to even manage it, and we sure as hell can't get it back once it has gone.

Knowing where you are on your life and business path is super important. Our goals, our dreams, our commitments, our energy levels, change as we get older... what we value often shifts too.

I don't want to work 20-hour days
I don't want to trade my time for money
I don't want to be managing a huge staff team
I don't want to be working until I am 87... that's how long I can expect to live for according to the Office for National Statistics.

I don't have the energy nor the patience for that

The average person in the UK will live for 80 odd years
That's around 960 months
4000+ weeks
29,000 days

I prefer to work in months, because I set monthly targets and I measure my metrics monthly. It also gives me 12 attempts at being successful each year, with a compounding accumulative effect.

If I think about progress in weeks I get overwhelmed, and daily huh, no chance.

The average person in the UK will have 40 odd years of productive working life in them...I know this varies, and I have plenty of clients well into their 60s that tell me off for using this graphic.

**WHERE ARE YOU NOW?**

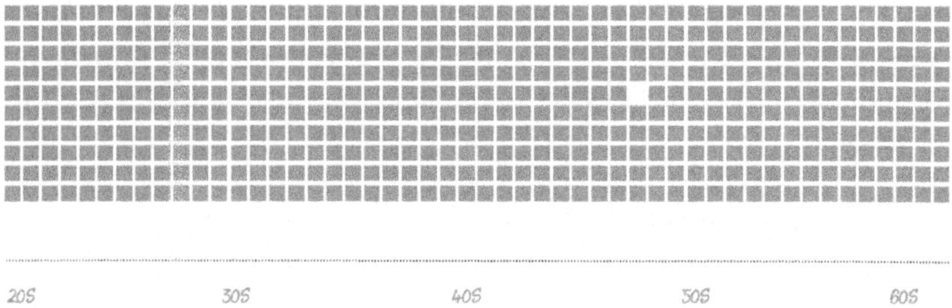

But most folks think about retirement around the 65 year mark...if their health or their energy reserves holds up that long, and lets face it some people don't even make it to their 40s, 50s, or 60s.

How does that make you feel, particularly in relation to wealth, or business success?

Do you feel like you have enough time left to do all the things you still want to do? Are you frustrated by the time you have already invested in your business, frustrated that you are not further ahead?

I get it.

When I was made redundant for the 5th time, having wound down both of my online businesses, I wasn't only sad or anxious because my income had completely dried up, I was annoyed and frustrated that I had wasted 6 months with this new company, AND I was determined to get myself back in the game ASAP because I know more than many how precious time is, and how important taking something new to market is.

I didn't have 2-3 years to build out a new brand, a new venture. I sure as hell didn't have the 10 years that it took for my plus size fitness business to be considered a leader in the industry.

*"What if I could do it in a year?"*

That's what I journaled on one morning.

What if all the changes I wanted to make in my life, I fast tracked them, got out of my own way by letting go of fear, overwhelm and procrastination.

I know how to build and scale businesses, I know how to take a creative idea and turn it into a profitable product or service, but could I do it at scale? Could I do it fast enough? And at the same time show others that it was possible?

That was when the idea for The Year to Change® came to me.

A methodology around productivity, focus and action.
An IP-able brand that would take my work from being a lifestyle business to a legacy business
A structure to incorporate the 3 strands of work that I do, personal, business and organisational change

And so, in the space of a week, I

- Worked with a kick arse designer to build out the visuals (I could have done this myself but procrasta-branding is a thing, and I needed another persons eyes on this for accountability)
- Created a DECK presentation that outlined my vision, the business plan, the brand, the revenue plan
- Secured a speaking gig with an audience of my peers and other solopreneurs for feedback
- And announced to the world my intention to rebuild my business and my life in just 12 months.

*"We overestimate what can be done in a year and underestimate what can be done in 10"* is often attributed to Bill Gates, the co-founder of Microsoft. I think it has also been claimed by various experts over the

years, but regardless of its precise origin, the sentiment behind the quote underscores the tendency for us to underestimate the long-term impact of consistent effort and progress while simultaneously overestimating the immediate results we can achieve in a short span of time.

This fits nicely too with "Parkinsons Law", which states that work expands to fill the time available for its completion. So, when we perceive we have ample time to do a task, we can procrastinate and become less focussed and efficient, whereas when we have limited time and a sense of urgency, suddenly it's like we have a rocket up our arse... but either way the job gets done.

This is where having ADHD hyper focus, AND leaving things to the last minute can sometimes work... just not with every aspect of business.

So, the question is... do you want to build your successful solopreneur business in a year, or 10 years... you decide which, because both are possible outcomes, depending on your starting point and the resources you have access to.

Don't get me wrong, there is a huge problem among solopreneurs having unrealistic expectations around what is possible, what progress can be made in short periods of time, that's why folks invest in all those "30 days to financial freedom" scams... because no one is ever really an overnight success, even if their rise to fame may appear so with the support of social media.

Things can often be done faster though.

I know that when my back is against the wall, when I am completely connected to a vision, when the alternative of impending doom doesn't bear thinking about, and when I have a well thought through plan, well, then miracles do happen.... and I can make shit happen -FAST.

I like to think of business traction in running terms

- Sprints
- Jogs
- Slogs...AKA Marathons

You will often hear people say: *"Business is a marathon not a sprint"* but let me tell you, having run 6 marathons, that is not the truth.

Building a successful business is much more akin to an ultramarathon, where you have all the pain and endurance of the marathon, but short bursts of walking and sprinting too, with no pressure to "Win" or even "Place" in comparison to anyone else... its simply not about that.

I once did a 24-hour ultramarathon. It was called The Spitfire Scramble and ran from 12 one day till 12 the following. Doing 6-mile laps, and returning to camp as often as you needed for sustenance, repair or camaraderie.

I did a few laps with other women from my community, and folks I knew from the running world...but most of it I did alone. Across the countryside of Essex, in the dark of night, tackling the hills, and the heat, and my inability to take on proper fuel.

7 laps I managed...doesn't sound a lot... but that totalled 42 miles, the furthest I had ever run, the longest I had ever been on my feet.

Isn't that more what business feels like? Never ending, but with real moments of pure joy and exhilaration? And a real sense of achievement when you look back at it?

The truth is we will have to be able to pick up the pace, and endure simultaneously... go fast AND slow, we need to let time run and momentum build, and we have to take action and make shit happen. That sometimes is the frustration, working out the right speed strategy, and managing your expectations about how fast things can happen for you.

We waste so much time by not focussing on the things that actually make a difference in business. We leave money and opportunity on the table by not taking fast action, due to the fear of getting it wrong or being judged, AND we give up on things that are working but just need more time.

Trial and error is a wonderful business strategy. But we must learn the lessons fast, and not repeat them too often. #notetoselfjulie

Too many solopreneurs stay firmly inside of their comfort zone, and take too long getting things to market, too long testing their products and services, too long getting in front of the right people, too long to pivot when things are clearly not working

Remember when the world went into lockdown, and overnight millions of businesses had to pivot. It was a scary time for sure, and many businesses didn't make it, but I saw so many absolutely thrive due to the fear of going under, due to the fear of not shifting online quick enough.... business owners who had been wanting to add digital products online, or group programmes delivered via Zoom for years... but just never found the time to do it.

I worked with 3000 clients during 2020... I made close to a quarter of a million pound, because of my ability to move fast, get out of my own way, and show others how to do this too.

6 months into launching the Year to Change® Brand I have

- Secured the IP (the intellectual property)
- Created a suite of concepts and models to use across the methodology
- Designed a number of MVPs (minimum viable products)
- Sold and tested that with more than 100 clients

- Used the brand to build out a number of other products and services
- Rebranded across all my social media channels
- Generated £50K of revenue
- Done the important longer term (3 year) strategy for building out the business into a million-pound, high impact venture
- Planned, wrote and published this book

Now I know it helps that I have a track record in developing online products and services, and an existing audience, but I have also had to do this without a working budget, and while building back my confidence and my health, which took a nose-dive, and while juggling being a solo parent in a new area.

I am seeing incredible results with my clients who are using the Year to Change® Methodology in both the personal development and business growth spaces, the work to take the methodology into organisations has been slower off the mark and so I am parking that until I have more capacity in the business to test it further.

So how does this work for you?

I think firstly you have to look at what it is you want to achieve in a year and why, and then you get to use the ready-made, pre-existing structure of a calendar year to plot it all out to include,

1 year – The BIG vision for exponential change
12 months – The roadmap for hitting key milestones
4 quarters – The measuring of metrics, and the tweaking of the plan
52 weeks – The micromanaging of your time and output
365 days – Self-awareness and discipline around preventing time and energy leaks

You also have to work out how much time realistically you have each week to work on, and in your business. You can totally have a sustainable thriving business working 10 hours a week, but only if you know you only have 10 hours a week, and only if you build out your strategy based on that.

Let's face facts, time is not equal for all of us

Who remembers the controversy when Love Islands Molly-Mae Hague, entrepreneur in her own right, caused chaos when she had the cheek to say *"We all have the same 24 hours in the day"* on Diary of a CEO podcast with Steven Bartlett

So, a few things on this.

Firstly, successful men have been saying *"We all have the same 24 hours a day"* for years, and it never created this amount of controversy; Molly was ripped to shreds on social media, which showcased how much misogyny still exists... I mean how dare a young woman be beautiful, smart, and rich, right?

But equally, it was a silly statement... we do not all have the same 24 hours in a day, and that comment, regardless of who it comes from, stinks of privilege.

If we take Molly as an example.

She is young and beautiful, and probably has more drive and determination to prove herself than most, meaning she has a whole heap of energy and determination to leverage her assets... she probably got some great advice before and after entering Love Island, meaning that opportunity acted like a springboard.

She has 7.7 million followers on Instagram... and an instagramable life that our image and aesthetic obsessed youth lap up.

She probably has a team, not only in her business but in her life to support her in raising her child, and she has a partner who is also wealthy, successful and in the public eye in his own right too

And this is before we talk about the other elephants in the room,

She is white
She is able bodied
She is (as far as I know) neuro typical

She is a marketer's dream, and I can only imagine the business opportunities that come to her, without her lifting a finger. She is set for life. And I am here for that 100%

Now this is not to take anything away from her as an astute business owner, she has worked hard, she has leveraged the resources and assets (lol) she had available to her... and let me say as an avid Love Island fan (oi don't judge me) she is still one of my all-time favourite guests.

But this isn't about Mollie Mae, it's about equality, fairness, and the access to opportunity. And it is about how we level the playing field when we don't ALL have the same 24 hours in a day... or unlimited youth, beauty, Instagram followers or access to money.

But we can't sit here and whinge... yeah and I know chances are you are off doom scrolling her gorgeous account, but come back, come back, it's time for you to work out how to leverage your most important resource too.

I set up my fitness business when Rose was incredibly small and time was precious. I had really short pockets of time to get things done, and not always a lot of energy, so that made me super-efficient.

Having never been a napper, the only time Rose ever slept during the day was if we went on a car ride, or occasionally in her pushchair after a long walk... I think boredom rather than tiredness is her sleep flex...and so I would leverage those extra pockets of time, and work from my parked car, or with her in the hallway in her pushchair... gaining me and extra 20 minutes here or there.

It was amazing what I could achieve in 2 short 20-minute blocks a day.

As Rose got older and life got more complex, running marathons and travelling more, I realised that keeping on top of my time was one of the few things I could control, and I developed a system to keep me motivated and focussed, and less likely to be distracted from bright shiny object syndrome... which is rife for us solopreneurs.

During the pandemic, time restraints became a thing again, and I needed to develop a system that ensured I only used my time for the important stuff, and so I developed a time management system called The Important Shit system... it took some time to implement it fully, but it was totally worth the effort.

Worth its weight in gold so to speak.

I split everything I do, or want to do, into 7 colours

- Red
- Green
- Yellow (GOLD)
- Pink
- Purple
- Blue
- White

I use a colour coded digital diary and a paper planner to sketch things out monthly, weekly and daily to keep on top of this. I don't use the system perfectly all of the time, but even if I uphold it 80% of the time, it keeps me super productive and organised.

Let me explain the colours briefly... what YOU choose to put on each list will be different... that's the fun bit

**Red - Shit List**

We all have things in our lives and business that are just shit to do, we don't like doing them, they take up our time, and we often put them off causing further issues down the line.

For me this is life admin, finance stuff, replying to emails, cleaning the house. I then allocate 2 times a week for me to do this, I don't want to be doing shit stuff every day as it sucks my energy. For me this works on Monday morning and Friday morning... it could be different for you.

Keep a check on how much Shit List stuff other people want from you, that don't really help you in anyway. What would happen if you said NO more? Plus how much of this could you outsource if you had more money?

**Green - Hit List**

This is the business of your business. This is the time you spend delivering what you deliver. But can also be other things you know you need to do consistently to grow your business, so marketing and sales could also sit here. I include any training I am doing, any regular meetings I attend, and any masterminds I am a part of.

Block out your week, and try not to multitask during these times... if most of your week is Green, we may have a problem. It is a good place to start so that you can see what is left for business development focussed tasks.

**Yellow - THE GOLD LIST**

THIS IS THE MOST IMPORTANT STUFF.

The thread of Gold through your working day, week, month and year is the thing that will build your business success.

It is often said that 80% of results, come from 20% of effort. So I want to see you blocking out at least 20% of your week for Gold List Tasks.

Gold list tasks are strategic, there are symbolic, they are structural, and they amplify you and your business. Again this will be different for different types of business owner, but these are often the things you know you want to do, know they would make a difference, but you rarely get round to them.

They are problematic because unlike other types of tasks you may have to be in the right frame of mind, or have the resources to move forward with them. They may require a learning curve, and be a project that takes several months... hence the reluctance to get started.

You need to schedule Gold List time in blocks of 60-90 minutes at a time, and when you are likely to have the most energy and the least distraction. You may also need to do some prep work so you have access to all the tools and information you need to get started.

Gold list tasks may require the support of another person, an expert to help drive the project forward.

You have to find a way for rewarding progress not completion, I award myself a gold star sticker every time I spend 60-90 minutes on a Gold List task, when I look back at my paper planner, I can see where business growth has come from... those little gold stickers.

Gold List tasks for me have included

- Writing a book
- Launching a podcast
- Redesigning my website
- Designing a new product
- Writing a social media strategy
- Recruiting a business manager

If you are not achieving 10 hours a month of Gold List activities most months...we need to talk!!!

## Pink

So, with all of that going on. When do you get an opportunity to actually do life? To do self-care? To exercise? To see friends? To have a love life? Well, if you are obsessive about your business as many of us are, often these are the things we sacrifice.

BLOCK this time out. Be present, not half there and half in your inbox. Sure, you can create content and use this to give folks a sneak peek into your life. But the biggest benefit of having a life outside of work is it reminds you why you are doing this, it replenishes your fuel supply, it reenergises, and reactivates you.

Pink stuff is good for the heart… it keeps you balanced.

## Purple - All things finance

This is a new addition to my system, and it is for all things finances. I used to put this under the Red…it was Shit List stuff for me, but what is that saying about how I view money? So, I committed to giving money stuff its own colour, its own energy… and I have already seen a shift. It helps that purple is the brand colour for this book… it's a reminder to practice what I preach.

I make little notes to chase invoices, or to check my balances, I have reminders to pay myself twice monthly…and seeing all those purple marks in my planner reminds me that money creates movement and momentum…and leads to magical things!!

I also block out Friday mornings for purple stuff.

## Blue - Reflection time

I need time away from business every now and again to strategize, to dream, to explore new ideas. To take a breather. This can be a short train ride, a 2-day conference, of a full-week's retreat somewhere… when I go without this for long periods of time, my creativity struggles, and I lose sight of the plan.

I schedule time at least quarterly for this, but ideally monthly...I include my CEO dates with myself in this bracket, and try to do this work away from my desk, in a nice café or an interesting venue.

It's that typical blue sky thinking energy.

It is connecting to your mission, your vision, your destined life path (without sounding too woo)

**White - What can other people do for me?**

There will come a day where you do not have enough time, energy or skill to do EVERYTHING, and you will have to outsource or bring in systems or processes to create efficiencies.

There are NEVER enough hours in the day to do it all.

I keep an ongoing white label list of things I want outsourcing, that I don't necessarily need to do myself but still needs to get done, (like my cleaning ha ha) and I sit with it. I can't always action it, but the list is there for when I have additional resources (money, time, creativity) to take action on finding a solution.

Outsourcing my cleaning was the first thing I did after my relationship breakdown...it was the best £20 a week I ever invested, freeing my up to make hundreds of pounds on a Monday morning, while Nina the Cleaner (seriously) worked her magic in my apartment.

**Grey - The colour I don't want to see**

There is one further colour in our system, Gray, but it doesn't feature much in my working week... I try to minimise this as much as possible (although I am human so sometimes slip up)

Grey is that wishy washy, ooops I just went off down a rabbit hole of shit that didn't make a difference to my business nor my life. It's doom scrolling on social media, it's fucking about with graphics, it's having meetings for no reason, it's developing things you know you will never take to market, it's organising files, it's attending events with no purpose....and guys, you NEVER get that time back, so please just don't sit in those Grey areas!!!!

Live your business life in full colour.

Whatever it is you want to achieve with your business this year, I guarantee you getting on top of your time and energy management, and blocking out your milestones and key dates will help you get there faster and with less stress.

Go back to the Where are you NOW graphic (above) and ask yourself, where do I want to be this time next year... and what do I need to do to ensure that is a possibility? I bet you the answer is in the Red, Gold and Green...its in the elimination of the Grey, doing more pink, taking time out for the blue, facing up to the purple.

How will you feel if nothing much has changed in a year? How will you feel if you go backwards?

In the journey of becoming a successful solopreneur and mastering the art of financial stability, time and energy management is a cornerstone principle, ignore it at your peril. As you work to build your brand, expand your client base, and optimize your operations, it's important to strike a balance between patience and urgency. Giving yourself time, but not too much, is a delicate equilibrium that can profoundly impact your financial trajectory.

So, while patience is vital, it's equally important not to succumb to complacency, which we will talk through in our next chapter about staying hungry once you find success, because we all know what happens when we have too much time or money on our hands right?

And I for one have no desire to fly to the moon in a rocket or to buy a remote island.

### How NOT to be Broke Top Tip

Understand how much time you REALLY have to work on your business, and get militant around how you use it.

Employ time blocking in a way that works for you, review and tweak this frequently to make the most of this important resource... if you have staff, or even family support members, ensure they know your system too.

Learn about how you waste time, through second guessing yourself or procrastinating... and work with that, not against it. Use body doubling, an accountability coach, digital and analogue tools to support you.

Try out my time blocking system... if nothing else please prioritise those GOLD List items and buy yourself some gold sticky stars.

**Entrepreneur (n.)**

1828, "manager or promoter of a theatrical production," reborrowing of French entrepreneur "one who undertakes or manages," agent noun from Old French *entreprendre* "undertake" The word first crossed the Channel late 15c. (Middle English *entreprenour*) but did not stay. Meaning "business manager" is from 1852.

CHAPTER 10

# DON'T LOSE YOUR APPETITE FOR CHANGE

***The financial landscape and opportunities in business change with time. Stay adaptable. Continuously update your knowledge, be open to new financial tools or strategies, and don't be afraid to pivot when necessary.***

I will never forget walking Rose to school on the last day before the COVID lockdown in the UK happened, in the spring of 2020. We had done the same 4 minute walk many times over the previous 3 years, always full of laughter and chatter...sometime setting intentions for the day ahead.

*"Today is going to be a goooooooood day..."* we would proclaim.

But today was a sad day. A day filled with fear and apprehension.

The mood was unsurprisingly tense around the school building, COVID in the middle of East London was no joke, by this point my family GP Dr Patel had already succumbed to the virus through excessive viral load, so the fear was real and tangible.

Parents mainly seemed to be avoiding eye contact as well as human contact...the teachers at the gates looked terrified. What was most scary was the prospect of having to home school my 6-year-old indefinitely while also trying to run two online businesses from home.

As we approached the school gate, paying attention to the temporary markings that had been in place to keep us a meter apart from one another (which was super difficult considering the school had over 1000 students) Rose started to cry.

I leant down and gave her a hug and asked *"What's the matter?"*

Her response, and FYI she was totally serious and totally distraught at this point,

*"You are going to have to teach me maths"*

Now the irony is not lost on me that I am writing a book about money, and I am shite at maths. I failed my GCSE maths twice, and often get my numbers mixed up... even now.

She was right... teaching maths was one of the hardest things I had to do during lockdown... but we got through it, and we laugh about it now.

Like most people the world over, the pandemic threw an absolute spanner in the works for my small business. The previous year had been a good year, my 3rd in a row six figure business revenue year, which was huge for a solopreneur like me, a solo parent like me, but 2020 was going to be my year of exponential growth.

I was going BIG.

Didn't know how... sure as hell didn't know a global pandemic would be the thing to unlock wealth in extraordinary amounts, but that's what happened.

I made more money than I knew what to do with in 2020.

It was an incredible year of doing what I do best, supporting others, creating new programmes and products (I think there were 15 new things in total), and inspiring folks to work with the resources they have at hand.

I even managed after the initial lockdown ended to fly off to a Greek island for 8 weeks to write my first business book, Leading from the Back, which took my business to even higher heights.

I think a lot of my success came from the initial fear of my business collapsing. It came from that typical fight or flight energy... that felt so familiar to me. Maybe even a little bit of "God Complex" believing I could REALLY help folks through this challenging period.

I ended the year having attracted (AKA worked my arse off for) over a quarter of a million pound in sales. I remember telling my brother in the pub after coming back from Greece that I had made £30K in a single month... he is a plumber so he's not short of a few bob himself, but I worried he would judge me.

Instead he said,

*"Fucking hell sis, that's brilliant... right I guess that makes it your round"*

The money wasn't the thing though.

The real thing was that I had finally achieved the freedom and autonomy that I had been striving for. In many ways I felt like it was the validation I had been looking for too. A justification of all the hard graft over the years. I had 2 businesses that were profitable, and purpose led. I had an audience of fans and supporters. I had found my flow in terms of marketing myself, and being visible online.

I had arrived.

In early 2021 I had my first ever 6 figure launch.

I had become one of those people.

One of those people who used their income as proof of their worth, proof of their ability to transform, proof that I was worth listening to, watching out for, trusting.

But can you see the problem with all of that?

It can be easy to start believing that hype yourself, to start believing that your worth is connected to the money you make... and guess what happens when you have a down month, a launch that doesn't go well, a month where you don't want to sell?

By January 2021, the time that the new social media platform Clubhouse had come on the scene, I was all over it, finding new audiences, being able to monetise my expertise with ease. I was totally in flow with making money, filling my programmes, raising my profile...I made around £10K from it in the first couple of weeks.

But with that increase profile also came increased pressure and stresses.

The *"more money, more problems"* lyric and the warning of *"pride always comes before a fall"* coming right to the fore.

I started getting inbox messages from more established business coaches questioning my ethics. A very well know coach accused me of stealing one of her programme names, when it was clear from historic social media posts, that I had named mine months before she took hers to market... didn't stop her legal threats and a blasé message of,

*"Doesn't matter who had the name first, I have more money than you, so if I take you to court, I will win"*

Well, that told me.

Another coach, this time someone I had worked with many years prior, did something similar, with the ever so funny voice note of,

*"Yeah I grew up on a council estate too you know, I'm not afraid to fight you on this"* which still makes me laugh... I am so not a fighter, but I know a fair few people who would literally pay money to see us both scrap lol.

I was seeing a lot of backlash in the online space from people buying programmes and not getting the results, lots of people in burnout, a lot of online bullying, a lot of fear and mistrust. Remember many solopreneurs had taken out Bounce Back loans in 2020, online coaches were genuinely encouraging their followers to do so, to pay for coaching... many of those same individuals are still struggling to pay those off now.

I was burning the candle at both ends. I was running a daily business breakfast show 6-8am, and then doing the school run, and then doing a whole days work. I was also still recovering from the impact of the Pandemic, doing too little in person work, and not really having much of a social life.

I was making all of this money, but the stress of it just wasn't worth it... I was spiralling into hopelessness because it never quite felt like it was enough, not enough to change the one thing that I really wanted to do, which was move out of London.

I ended up pulling the plug on a whole heap of my coaching programmes, and just retreated into my cave. I was in burnout, emotional and physical burnout... I had lost my direction of travel, my true north star.

The money just simply wasn't enough.

Which I know was OK for me to say, given the bumper 18 months I'd just had, and the reserves I had built up. I knew I was in a position of privilege to be able to take my foot off the gas for a while. This isn't always the case for everyone, it hadn't always been the case for me.

Behind the scenes I was simultaneously investing in infrastructure, new branding and a team... something my then coach told me I had to do. I recruited a part time business manager at great stress, overwhelm and expense, the whole thing becoming probably the most costly thing I have ever done in business.

The lady in question was lovely and highly skilled, and she really tried to understand and systematise my business. But I didn't need a manager... managing me is like managing jelly, in a tumble drier, with a cheese grater thrown in for fun.

I didn't fully understand the extent of my ADHD back then, and I found myself bending over backwards to fit systems that actually stunted my creativity and growth, rather than supported it.

It was 6 months of absolute hell and probably saw me throw close to £50K down the pan, and who knows what money I left on the table by not leveraging the growth and momentum of the previous year effectively... and then I got COVID.

Like are you shitting me?

I had just allowed my nervous system to come back down to earth after the disruption of all the lockdowns, home schooling and all that glorious stuff. I was just about keeping my shit together... I couldn't cope with having to ramp things up again after an extended illness.

I was sick of bouncing back at this point...ten steps forward, 10 back, rinse and repeat...something always tying me back to hardship and challenge. Some might call it Sods Law, bad luck, a curse.

Turns out, it is just life.

Oh and maybe a bit of a tug from my ancestors lol

Prior to getting the Covid, I had taken myself off on a mini business retreat to get some headspace... some of that glorious blue sky thinking time, and to give my body and soul a chance to recover and reconnect with my vision... which was most needed.

I had an amazing 5 days with an incredible coach (and peer) Kate Taylor, in sunny Ibiza, eating vegan food, swimming in the ocean and practicing Qoya a form of movement that enables you to work through your emotions physically... it was incredible, unlocking so much, and giving me time to think about what I wanted out of business and I headed back to the UK with a plan.

The plan however did not include getting COVID on the plane home.

What started off with a tickly cough and fatigue as I tried to adjust to solo parenting and being back in London, turned into me literally not being able to move.

Rose went to her Dads, and I spent a week feeling incredibly sorry for myself.

I cried when a neighbour who I had never met in my block, left a huge bag of Ginger on my doorstep, with a note that said "hope this helps"

I cried again when I realised I had no cold drink in the house, and I couldn't get my ApplePay working on my phone (as I had misplaced my bank card) so couldn't even order a Deliveroo... sad, sad times.

Then just when I thought I was starting to get better, I walked my antibodies test to the post-box, my first outside trip in 10 days, and when I returned I felt like I literally couldn't catch my breath...the next thing I knew I was being whisked away in an ambulance with all the lights and sirens where I would spend a night on a trolly in a corridor in Homerton Hospital.

Now not to be too dramatic... but I thought I was going to die.

I didn't, obviously, as here I am writing this book, but at the time it felt so tangible... I laugh now, that even in that place of despair, I still felt the need to update my audience, posting a black and white (for aesthetic purposes) photo of me hooked up to oxygen... truth was I didn't want to die alone.

And as I lay there imagining the worse, with nothing much else to occupy my mind seeing as it was 2am and my phone battery had now died, I saw the movie of my life. It had been a good life. A blockbuster hit. One of adventure, and fun, and incredible experiences. I had done more in my 43 years of life than most.

I'd travelled the world.
I'd climbed mountains and run marathons... 5 by then.
I'd rubbed shoulders with prime ministers, and global sports stars, and even met the Queen...and Carrie from Sex in the City
I'd helped millions of people to make changes in their lives.
I'd won awards, published books, given closing keynotes.
I'd been to gala dinners, opening nights, closing parties.
I'd done a lot.
I'd endured a lot
I'd overcome a lot

But ultimately it wasn't enough.

All I could think about was how I hadn't left enough for Rose, my then 8 year old.

I hadn't prepared her for a life without me, I hadn't equipped her, I hadn't left enough of an estate to keep her safe and secure, to ensure she didn't end up living an early life of poverty just like I had.

I hadn't spent enough time playing with her, I'd taken too many holidays with business buddies while chasing my dream, I'd spent too many weekends at conferences trying to build my profile.

What had it all been for?

I had regrets.

Regrets that I had cared so much about what other people had thought of me. Regrets that I hadn't been more careful with my money, more strategic, more measured. Regret that I had put off doing charitable work... because I thought I still had time, and that I would do something like that when I was rich.

It was a lot.

And that's when I started to pray.

Not to God...no, those days were well and truly over.

But to me... there goes that God Complex again... no but it was a promise, a promise that never again would I second guess myself.

If I lived (I know, dramatic much?) I would take every opportunity... win or lose.

I'd make bolder steps. I'd take the leap. I would show Rose what living in the NOW looks like. I would say yes to the dates, I would say yes to the holidays, I would dance in the rain with Rose, we would move out of London, by hook or by crook.

That's when the ever so handsome doctor came into the corridor and told me I could go home. My chest X-rays had come back fine, my oxygen levels were back to normal, what I had experienced was more of a panic attack and I could expect to be OK in a few days with lots of rest.

Phew.

Now I had to bloody well follow through with all those things I had committed to.

The following week... when I was feeling totally back to my old self, I was hosting a 2-day business retreat in East London, Abseiling off the highest structure in Europe with a handful of my clients.

Yeah right back into the thick of things.

The week after that I was at the launch event of a new film about Ultra Running by Olympian Ewan Thomas, where, by chance, I got speaking to another running bloke who told me about the Sierra Leone Marathon... deemed the craziest marathon on the planet.

6 months later, I was boarding a plane to Freetown, with 5 clients to undertake the biggest adventure of my life... running a full-blown marathon, in 30 degree heat and 90% humidity...in an attempt to raise £100,000 for the Charity Streetchild.

I don't do bounce back by halves... I don't bounce back... I don't know about you, but I am not travelling backwards, been there done that, I bounce forward, into the future, with renewed enthusiasm, renewed curiosity, and renewed gratitude that I am still on this planet, living out my purpose.

Looking at how I manage to come back from adversity over and over again, I realised that I intuitively follow a process. A process that has been present through every low point of my life, career, business... even in my disastrous relationships.

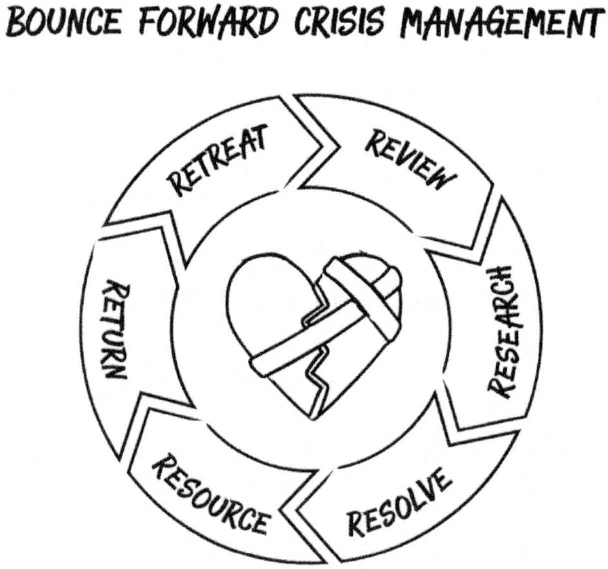

You have to learn to retreat in business. To literally take yourself away from the things which are causing you stress and pain. You can't fix a mess while 100% enveloped by it...space gives you perspective.

The review part, is an opportunity for self-reflection, for looking at the metrics, for taking radical responsibility, and not playing the blame or shame game for too long.

The research is about identifying potential solutions and not just jumping in with the first thing that comes to mind... the asking yourself "I wonder if... and I wonder how..." being open to new ways of doing things, knowing that an opportunity to change your life and your business could be just around the corner.

Having the resilience the resolve to give it another go, takes courage. It takes energy. You have to be sure that it's worth it. For me this is about getting clear on what needs to be different.

Most problems that need fixing need resourcing, whether that be time, money, attention or other people. So make sure you are coming from a place of resource, rather than lack before going again.

And only then do we make our return, when grounded, when confident of a way forward.

This stops us from jumping from crisis to crisis to crisis.

You can use this tool after a disappointment, a challenging period, when your team expands, even with family stuff that comes up. It creates space to think things through and pause before being reactive to problems.

The Sierra Leone trip helped me to bounce forward with great gusto, I felt connected to my purpose again. It stopped me from living in the past and the future, and showed me the power I had to make change NOW.

I always thought I had to be rich and famous to make a difference.

I thought I would have to start a foundation, or be awarded an MBE, or raise millions for charity before I could be considered a philanthropist, a change maker... the truth is, that is the biggest pile of bullshit.

We are ALL changemakers, and you do not need to have money to enable change.

Look an Ghandi
Look at Malala
Look at Mother Teresa

For sure you can use your money for good too, nothing wrong with a bit of check book philanthropy... but do not use a lack of money as an excuse for not making a difference... there is always a way of giving, of sharing, of changing the world for the better.

We didn't hit our target of raising £100,000

We raised just short of £20,000 in the end, but the PR coverage we got in relation to our African adventure, the hearts and minds that we affected through our endurance at that event... that was priceless.

And what it has led to is an ongoing partnership, where I commit indefinitely to support that charity however I can, whether that be as an ambassador, as a fundraiser, as a donor.... I will raise £100K.

Streetchild exists to improve education for children and young people in some of the hardest environments in the world, from Sierra Leone to Ukraine, responding to war, environmental disasters and neglect.

They use entrepreneurship as the vehicle for change, upskilling local women in the community to start up super-micro businesses, which fund putting their children through school.

Find out more about the work of Streetchild at www.street-child.org

We take it for granted in the Western World that education is free, of reasonable quality, and part of the expected trajectory when it comes to success. But let's not forget it hasn't always been that way, especially not for the working classes, especially not for women.

My Great grandmother received no schooling.

My nan left education at the age of 8...bullied because of her surname Jerman (at the height of tensions preceding the 2$^{nd}$ world war)

My mum did typing at school, a sure-fire way to secure a job after leaving secondary school, for a girl from her background.

And let's not forget Education literally saved my life growing up... a good few teachers believing in me, and the opportunity to go to college to do something creative, and then on to higher education, without my parents having to fund it.

I had a chance at life.

So many of the children I met around the streets of Makeni in Sierra Leone, did not. With less than 50% literacy rate... yet almost 100% mobile phone ownership... there is so much potential, and yet so much work that still needs to be done to level the playing field.

We cannot welcome the best of globalisation and ignore the bits that are challenging. We each have a responsibility to address the inequalities we see at home and abroad, to make this world a fairer place, and money and business are both incredible ways of making a start.

So, when you think ah *"It doesn't matter if I don't make much money from my business"* just think about what good you could do with the excess, the causes you could support, the employment you could create... the safety net you can create for yourself and your loved ones.

It is easy to think that making enough money in your solopreneur business signals the end of any challenges you face. This is not true. It's not a case of more money, more problems, but a case of more money, different problems; though having access to money often gives you better options for solving those challenges....you ever tried to fix a broken washing machine with good will?

Money mindset expert Denise Duffield Thomas says,

*"New Level, New Devil"*

And it's true, at each level of growth, be that financial, spiritual, emotional or physical... you will be required to reinvent yourself... to continually ask yourself *"what is it I want?" "What is my purpose here?" "How can I be of service?"*

So many people acquire wealth and then lose it all because the new experience of abundance feels uncomfortable. They don't have a strong enough sense of who they are with money, what they can do with their new wealth, they can't see the endless possibilities for living a life filled with purpose that having excess money affords you.

We need to get better at articulating our desires, going after what we want.

My all-time favourite coaching exercise is one that I developed around a decade ago called 12 in 12, which I have used with thousands of my clients over that time... and was perhaps the precursor to The Year to Change® Methodology

It started off simple.

I asked myself what 12 things I want to achieve in the next 12 months. I allowed myself a few minutes to write the list and then I challenged myself to get as many of these items ticked off as possible.

I then questioned why I had to do all the hard graft... and wondered if the universe, or anyone else who was listening, could meet me half-way, what would happen if I publicly shared my list. The results the second time round were much better.

The less my list looked like a To-Do list, the more exciting it became. The more expansive my desires become. I allowed myself to dream bigger, to get more specific, to be open to good things happening.

I learned to release some of the shame and embarrassment I felt about having some things.

I also moved the timelines to 12 weeks... why did I have to wait a whole year for good things to happen? What if they started happening sooner than that, what if I could get more of what I wanted in the next 3 months...that would ensure I took more action right?

I use this tool with my clients, and I use it religiously myself as a way of checking in with my desires. I tend to get around 5-6 of the things listed in the 12 weeks, and some roll over 2 or 3 periods before they come through... or they stay on the list as a reminder of the harder things I am working towards.

Some things fall off my list altogether as I realise I don't actually want them.

One of the rules I set with clients though is the list must be about them, they can't desire things on behalf of other people, for their partners, their kids, their clients. This list is about them, I want them to get selfish.

Once you have an abundance of what you want... then there is capacity to help others.

You cannot fill from an empty cup.

You cannot change the world, when your world is falling apart.

And so.

When the shit hits the fan, or you find yourself at a loss for what to do next?

Figure out what it is you want.

Then.

Retreat, Review, Research, Resolve, Resource, and then, and only then Return.

Always moving forward, always acknowledging your power as the ultimate change maker in your life. We never give up; we just learn how to connect back to our vision for who we are and what we came here to do.

And remember boredom, complacency, inertia...they are types of crisis too!!!

## How NOT to be Broke Top Tip

Do the 12 in 12 exercise and see what magic happens over a 12-week time frame.

Explore what comes up emotionally for you about what you are allowed to have. What action you take towards receiving the things on your list... what resistance you have to asking for what you truly desire.

Share your 12 in 12 with me if you want an extra bit of accountability julie@juliecreffield.com or send me a DM on socials using the hashtag #iblamejulie or #notbroke.

**legacy (n.)**

late 14c., *legacie*, "body of persons sent on a mission," from Medieval Latin *legatia*, from Latin *legatus* "ambassador, envoy, deputy," noun use of past participle of *legare* "send with a commission, appoint as deputy, appoint by a last will" (see legate) Sense of "property left by will, a gift by will" appeared in Scottish mid-15c.

CHAPTER 11

# *CREATING A LASTING LEGACY*

***Legacy is how you live NOW. The choices you make today shape the legacy you leave behind, and not just for your own bloodline. Instead of waiting for "someday," act now. Live by the values, habits, and financial decisions you want to be remembered for, the values, habits and financial decisions that leave the planet, and humanity as a whole, better for you having been born.***

NO PRESSURE HEY?

Ok, to let's go back a bit.

Can we just take a moment to remember how we got here, all of the things which had to transpire across time and space for you to come into existence, to have reached the ripe old age you have. Can we take a moment to think about the generations that came before us, that fought so hard to afford us the luxuries of choice and freedom we have... even if at times it feels like we are going backwards in some respects.

Can we all just take a moment.

Amelia Jerman was my great grandmother. I never met her, but I very much wish I had. Goodness me the questions I would have asked that woman. She lived in the East End of London and had 18 children. No. You didn't read that wrong. Eighteen.

I cannot imagine being responsible for that many human beings. Can you imagine the laundry? The food bill?

When collating some photos to make a video montage for my Nans wake, I came across a number of photos of my great grandmother, possibly for the first time. She was absolutely beautiful. Like a doll. The first photo I have of her she looked so young, just out of her teens perhaps. She is sitting in a chair with my great grandfather standing to her right, and my great uncle Les (my nans brother) just below her...he would have been aged 3 or so, he was her 9th child.

My great grandpa was in his army uniform, Amelia, a slim dark-haired lady, was in a full-length black skirt with a long sleeve white blouse and a simple pendant necklace around her neck. There is a sadness to the photo, which I understand was how photos were taken back then... no smiling or goofy selfies, just solemn, respectable records of your existence. But perhaps she was sad... who knows.

I wonder if she knew she would go on to have so many more children, I wonder if she believed that some time in the distant future, women would have more choice when it comes to reproduction and child baring?

A later photo of her showed a very different type of woman, robust, rotund... in today's world we would maybe even describe her as plus sized. Her teeth, which hadn't been shown in the first photo, in this one appeared to be misshapen, her clothes not to pristine. But she was smiling.

My Mum told me a story about her nan once learning to play the ukulele. I had popped to see my Mum to pick up some jewellery of my Nans she was decluttering, we stood there in her open plan kitchen in Chelmsford, and I remembered the small kitchenet where my nan used to feed 10 people, where she was still doing laundry by hand.

My Mum opened up a bit about her childhood.... something she didn't do very much. My mum had lived with her nana and grandad for a while... her grandpa had been a bit of a mean man by all accounts.

But the ukulele???

Who has eighteen children and still finds the energy to go and learn an instrument? It literally blows my mind. It almost feels like a middle finger to the patriarchy and the lunacy of having so many children... it also makes me think of George Formby's When I'm Cleaning Windows

Amelia had eighteen children (sorry I know I keep banging on about it)
My Nan, Silvia had eight
My Mum, Janice had 6

And I had just the one... one is quite enough, thank you very much.

I am not sure if it was my plan to keep my own family small, I knew I wanted children, I just didn't want as many as my mum. I remember the fear I felt when Rose was about a year old and her dad suggested we had another child, the idea was preposterous to me. We had no money, no job between us, we were not eligible for any support with the mortgage, to be fair we weren't even getting on any more, and here he was wanting to procreate again.

No thank you .

I've heard my Mum say she should have stopped after one, which means I would never have been born. But I understand her reasoning, my Dad was already showing signs that he would be a useless father. Leaving a problematic relationship gets harder the more children you have with a person right?

I come from a long line of strong women who learned how to endure. It is quite literally in my DNA. As an endurance athlete I know about perseverance, putting in the training hours... being in it for the long haul, not peaking too soon, being hyper focussed and patient, learning to take the rough with the smooth. The pain, the grit, the determination.

But I also choose something different for myself for my life.

I love and totally respect my mum, my nan, my great grandma... they did the absolute best with the resources they had. They performed miracles, getting food on the table, and clothing and entertaining so many children simultaneously. They raise hard working, honest human beings who in turn have done the same.

But they left very little for themselves.

They were Martyrs, frustrated with their lives and with regrets I am sure.

I don't want that life for me, and I don't want that life for my own daughter.

They had an abundance of children, a wealth of laughter, and love and memories...but they also had fewer choices than me when it comes to life opportunities, health and wellbeing, and autonomy to do the things they really wanted to.

They put their kids first no doubt, but there is always a cost when there are so many other people to care for... and often it is the women that bear the brunt of that... and I am not sure much has changed in that respect.

I choose something different.

I choose to change the trajectory of my own life, to inspire future generations that they can decide on different pathways too if they should so wish.

My Mum always told us that she wanted to study Criminal Law, I feel sad that she has never managed to do so... she could have done when we had all grown up, but by that time she had so many health conditions and a general lack of confidence that she never pursued it.

That makes me sad.

It also reminds me of that time where I thought I was dying and had regrets, and my determination to address those feelings before it was too late.

Bronnie Ware is an Australian nurse turned blogger, wrote a book in 2012 called *The Five Regrets of The Dying*, she said the collation of the stories brought her to tears, and when I look at this list I am in total agreement

1. **I wish I'd had the courage to live a life true to myself, not the life others expected of me. "**this was the most common regret of all. When people realise that their life is almost over and look back clearly on it, it is easy to see how many dreams have gone unfulfilled. Most people had not honoured even a half of their dreams and had to die knowing that it was due to choices they had made, or not made. Health brings a freedom very few realise, until they no longer have it."
2. **I wish I hadn't worked so hard.** Interestingly "This came from every male patient that I nursed. They missed their children's youth and their partner's companionship. Women also spoke of this regret, but as most were from an older generation, many of the female patients had not been breadwinners."
3. **I wish I'd had the courage to express my feelings.** "Many people suppressed their feelings in order to keep peace with others. As a result, they settled for a mediocre existence and never became who they were truly capable of becoming. Many developed illnesses relating to the bitterness and resentment they carried as a result."

4. **I wish I had stayed in touch with my friends.** "Often they would not truly realise the full benefits of old friends until their dying weeks and it was not always possible to track them down. Many had become so caught up in their own lives that they had let golden friendships slip by over the years. Everyone misses their friends when they are dying."
5. **I wish that I had let myself be happier.** Many did not realise until the end that happiness is a choice. They had stayed stuck in old patterns and habits. The so-called 'comfort' of familiarity overflowed into their emotions, as well as their physical lives. Fear of change had them pretending to others, and to their selves, that they were content, when deep within, they longed to laugh properly and have silliness in their life again."

A big driver for me in life is not having regrets.

I don't mind the failure, the knockbacks, the things that didn't work out, because I try, I have big ambitions, big dreams. I take on challenges, and go on adventures, I am an explorer at heart... I want to know when I go, that I have given life and all it has to offer a good shot.

Many of these things come at a cost though... they quite literally cost money.

But there are other ways too. My businesses have enabled me to travel, to undertake challenges, to explore new ideas. I have made friends all over the world.

I will never forget the time I flew to Cape Town to speak at a conference. It was my first international speaking gig and the whole trip was amazing, on the final day before I flew home, one of the delegates, a lovely Muslim lady called Huni who I had met just that day, asked me if I would like to spend my remaining time with her to see the "Real Cape Town" away from the beach side luxury hotel we were staying in.

Well, you know the answer to that.

With Huni I got to visit the nearby Townships, we visited female empowerment projects, a local social enterprise, a pop-up boutique coffee shop, and then she invited me that evening into her home for dinner, to meet her family and to enjoy home-made Chai Lattes before she dropped me back to my accommodations so I could fly home.

Priceless.

We often think that legacy is about the financial assets we leave our kids. Of course, those things are important. Many parents of previous generations worked tirelessly to provide stable homes, and then left those to their children to help them build their own lives.

But legacy isn't just about that.

Our lives are our legacy. The things we choose, and the things we don't. The examples we leave, the stories, the adventures, the way we make people feel.

Our legacy is how we raise our kids, how we support other peoples kids, how we nurture our communities, deal with work colleagues, engage with strangers. It is how intentional we decide to be in changing what is within our own control... like a simple smile, or not assuming the worst of people.

Our legacy is our life's work for sure, but also it's our story, how we navigated our own lives, sometimes intertwined with business accolades, and professional highlights... but more so the day-in day-out way that we treat ourselves and others.

We get to write that story.
We get to write that history.
And our businesses can be an incredible enabler in writing the chapters of our life in exciting inspiring ways, if we allow them to.

Be. Do. Have. Give. Teach

That is my life motto.

Be who you want to be
Do the things which inspire you.
Have all the things which make your soul happy
Give willingly to others
Teach (or share) the lessons to inspire others

And I couldn't write about legacy without mentioning the man who came into my life when I was 10 years old who changing the whole trajectory of my life.

It was the mid-eighties and I was at a family wedding. Madonna's Material Girl (oh the irony) was blasting out in the background. I was wearing my best dress, lace gloves and dangly earrings in the shape of high heel shoes, and in the crook of my arm proudly sat the first hand-bag I ever owned... I thought I was IT.

My Nan, Sylvia... but always referred to as Nanny Silver, was literally my favourite person in the world back then, she had told me that her brother Les, would be coming to the wedding, and that I should try and spend some time with him if I could... she had a feeling we would get on.

My uncle Les was a journalist for The Scotsman newspaper, and we bonded over our shared love of words.

I had always loved words.
I loved how they made me think and feel and understand the world.
They helped me to process my thoughts, and express the chaos in my mind.

Mostly though I loved how they helped me to escape, escape the challenges of growing up in my working-class household, a household filled with arguments, and noise, and fights over who had the most fish fingers, and what to watch on the TV.

After being introduced as "Jan's eldest girl"

I boldly told him,

*"I'm Julie, and I want to be a writer too when I'm older"*

And his response, without as much as a shred of sarcasm?

*"Well... if you want to be a writer, then we must get you writing"*

And with that he reached into the inside pocket of his tweed jacket, pulled out a small notepad and a pen which felt like they had been placed there specifically for this moment in time.

He scribbled on the paper furiously, ripped off the note like it was a prescription, folded it in half and handed it to me across the sticky table, nodding towards my handbag as if to say put it away so you don't lose it.

*"You will become my Pen Pal Julie, and we will correspond until the day you do indeed become a writer"*

And that was that.

I never believed it could be possible for a girl like me to become a writer, because despite how much I loved reading and writing, I didn't feel like anyone would ever care enough about what I had to say, I was too insignificant, not smart enough, not well mannered enough... plus surely I'd have to get a real job at some point.... or worse still get married. Ewwwwww!

But for 15 years, off the back of that inaugural meeting years we would indeed correspond, and he didn't even mind about my grammar, my poor spelling, or even the ridiculously inane things I'd tell him about.

When I went off to Uni, there was an envelope waiting for me on the table of my halls of residence, the short note read "For books and a few drinks" and there was a cheque for £500. Nobody had ever given me that much money before in my life. What would he want in return was my immediate thought, followed by "I'd better not tell my siblings, they will all want £500 in the post too"

Uncle Les never minced his words, he said things as they were, never refraining from telling me about his annoying prostate, or how much he hated the fuss of Christmas as he got older, or what was wrong with the criminal justice system... a big passion of his after pleading with a judge to free the burglar who had broken into his house, stating, "they are only possessions, this is a man's life we are talking about here your honour"

Every publication, every blog post, every article, every social media post I have ever put out into the world, that is in part due to his legacy, his legacy of support, encouragement and investment in me, alongside of course the legacy he created in his own right as a journalist, with thousands of articles. A reported 12,000 entries in the London Evening Standard, earning the title, the King of the Fleet Street Diarists.

It was the year after he passed that I started writing my blog the Fat Girls Guide to Running, reflecting now, I wonder if I started those diary entries because I missed having someone to write to about how I was feeling. At the time I never imagined my words would have such impact... I think the first blog was initially ready by 12 people...5 of whom were my siblings.

At its height tens of thousands of women read each post.

I never shared my thoughts on being overweight with Uncle Les, nor my inner fears about being judged as a writer. I don't think he would have cared much for either of those concerns. I always shared with him though, what I was currently reading, and what I was thinking about or exploring, and he would do the same... in the later years he would often repeat himself, and send me the same photocopied articles and sketches from his back catalogue... I never mentioned this to him though.

I often wonder what he would have made of my online writing and the books I have gone on to publish, especially this one.

*"If you want to be a writer, you must write"* he said on a post card, when I pressed him about writing a book someday.

My early writing via that blog is where it all started. That blog helped me to create an online platform with my words being read by millions, my story shared in more than 50 countries, translated into languages I can't even decipher. Being given the title of influencer, change maker, campaigner... my writing leading to international travel, sponsorship deals and high-profile speaking gigs.

Just my words.

Les was the original blogger... long before digital blogging was a thing. In fact I am not sure he ever owned a computer, "terrible things" he once told me, when I wrote to him to tell him I was using the university's computer room to write my letters to him these days, he liked it when I put pen to actual paper... even if he himself preferred his trusted typewriter with fountain pen notes in the margins.

One day, a few years before his death, whilst I was scanning The Guardian for jobs, I found a letter entitled "Whatever happened to Leslie Jerman" reminiscing about his days as the King of Fleet Street.

I felt compelled not only to write to the Guardian to share that he was alive and kicking and still very much writing, but no longer visible in the UK press... but also, I cut out the clipping and popped it in the post to Les with a brief hand-written note...

*"Still enjoying your name in print?"*

We live in an age now where there are no real barriers to writing. Billions and billions of words are created and published every day, billions and billions more stay locked away in unfinished manuscripts, and half written blog posts.

Finding your voice in business, written or spoken, is one of the biggest investments you can make. If you have something you want to express, you can just get out there and say it. My words have encouraged folks to set up businesses, to start up movements, to go big, to take small but ever so important first steps towards greatness. My words have taken many of their fans to the extremes of human endurance, and way beyond the comfort zones which keep us playing small... and I make no apologies for that.

My words haven't always been high-falutin, or academic in their tone, shit, they have often been ranty, filled with bad language, and full of spelling errors and grammatical mistakes, but they have broken through the noise somehow.

My daughter has never known me not to write, when I die, she will have the unenviable task of clearing out the hundreds of diaries, notebooks and journals, filled with my frustrations, hopes and dreams for the future.

At my Brother's wedding a few years back my niece Ruby turned to me and said,

"Auntie Julie, I know what it is you do"
"Go on" I encouraged with a smirk... it had been a long-standing joke with her trying to figure out what I actually did for a living
"You teach people the way of life, innit?" to which me and my sister started giggling uncontrollably, which caused my Mum to shusssshhh us as the bride was about to make her entrance.

You see how this stuff goes full circle.

My words are my legacy.

Now your legacy as a business owner doesn't need to be about your words. It may be about your actions. It may be about the lives you change, how you make people feel. It might be the contribution you make to the household bills, it might be the things you fight for and against.

Now this is all well and good...but surely your legacy is years away.

You have to deal with the challenges of today. But don't you see they are one and the same.

Tomorrow isn't promised, we can't be living in the future... your legacy is in the here and now, which is why becoming profitable, leveraging your existing resources and assets, knowing your worth, is so important.

We can't waste the opportunity that we have today... we can't put it off until tomorrow, because then we are just delaying our potential.

It's not a race, it's not a competition... we get to go at our own pace... but we have to stay in momentum, we have to keep making moves, even if some of them are sideways or even temporarily a little backwards.

But only with a plan... have a plan, have a view of where you want to end up, where you want the world to go after you depart this planet.

When you are clear on your purpose, you will find the right tactical solutions, you can work on your mindset, you can steadily grow your influence, these things flow out of your soul like water down a stream. When you don't have that clarity, it feels like no man's land, a battle-field, a swamp of no hope

But we don't need hope remember, we need a strategy... a strategy, a direction of travel and a commitment to communicate it as far and wide as you can, with your words and with your actions.

That Legacy Masterplan probably won't be linear, I mean how could it be? There will be levels that play out consciously and some that are totally subconscious, things within your control and things which seem to happen as if they were ordained.

Your action plans need to have more process and flow, but your heart centred vision of what you want to leave behind, that can take whatever format 2D, 3D or totally hypercomplex...matrix like in its application and aesthetic.

You don't need to be particularly spiritual or woo to connect to this, we can totally make this practical in its application, but in its most simplest form, it starts with intention, fuelled by belief, and is followed by action, and always with a sprinkling of magic

We cannot predict the future, we may not even be able to shape it totally to get what we want, but we can be intentional about how we wish it to look, we can bring people with us on that journey and move closer towards that vision.

Make today the day you step into that future version of yourself, the version of you where your great nieces and nephews want to sidle up beside you at family weddings, the version of you that gets spoken about behind your back (but in a good way obvs), and decades after you are no longer here.

Get started, do it imperfectly, share what is inside of you, because trust me the process will change you, and who knows it might even change the world... and no that is not too much, it's not even enough, for the shifts that need to happen.

## How NOT to be Broke Top Tip

Write your own obituary, what do you want said about you when you die, how do you want people to feel, what do you want to have left behind. This is a challenging exercise, but one which will hopefully give you clarity over what is important, in business and in life.

Think about the things you want in your life, think about how you can have more of that now. Rather than say, *"When my business is doing better, I will have monthly spa breaks"* schedule them into your diary and do them at home at low cost... lean into your future self, allow yourself to have more of what you want now.

If you are an experience business owner with a track record of success and tangible assets and resources behind you, but you know you need to do some work to secure this legacy piece? We should talk. Drop me a line julie@juliecreffield.com and let's see how we might cocreate this vision and start taking action.

Oh and a final idea..

I did this for each of my nieces and nephews a few years back. I call it the Golden Envelope Experience, whereby I gifted all 10 of my siblings children a gold envelope with a crisp £50 note.

This was 2020 the year of the pandemic, as we learned the news that we would all be having to stay at home on Xmas day.

Some of my older nieces and nephews would have most definitely received more than £50 before in Birthday money and gifts, but none of them had ever owned a £50 note, and the younger kids most definitely had never been handed that amount of money before.

It was fun.
It was expansive (if also a little expensive)
It was great seeing the looks on their faces (often behind a closed gate as we did door to door visits with social distancing in play)
But it was also great to see my siblings face

They knew I had a had a cracking year, and they were happy I was sharing the wealth.
I also made a hefty donation to my local food bank.
Who could you gift unexpected money to...with no expectation?
What legacy would that create?

**manifesto (n.)**

"public declaration explaining reasons or motives for a course of actions done or planned," 1640s, from Italian *manifesto* "public declaration explaining past actions and announcing the motive for forthcoming ones," originally "proof," from Latin *manifestus* "plainly apprehensible, clear, apparent, evident"

CHAPTER 12

# *THE HOW NOT TO BE BROKE MANIFESTO*

**To manifest means to bring something into existence.**

Manifestation is often believed to be done through the power of thought alone, I can assure you never have I ever been able to generate £10,000 just by thinking it into existence... and I think about money A LOT.

Manifestation is about thought, YES, but it is also about the frequency you emit, the action you take, and the trust and belief you have that what you want or something better is coming... so in other words patience.

I have been careful not to get too spiritual nor too scathing of the whole law of attraction approach to wealth creation in this book, but I want to in this penultimate chapter reinforce the concepts of this book and encourage you to set in place some activation points to keep you connected to your goals and vision for sustainable wealth creation.

If the Law of Attraction, vision boards, affirmations and the like help you get in the zone for making money, and prompts you to take action, great; if you think it is all bullshit, think more in terms of The Law of Cause & Effect.

Either way it starts with having a vision for what you want and a belief that it is possible, without that how do you know the direction of travel?

Then comes the creation of a strategy and an action plan for getting there, but with the caveat that the plan might change (and probably will) but the destination doesn't need to...not if you are committed to reaching a specific goal.

Then it's about staying on top of the things on a day-to-day basis, to keep your vibration high... so that you take inspired action, because I mean, who takes action when they are feeling like shite?

And then most importantly it is knowing that what is meant for you will find you, if you take enough inspired action, and know that you worth is unrelated to the external things that so many of us chase.

You will never be broke.

When it comes to the material trappings of wealth, the cars, the holidays, the Instagramable homes, sure have them if that stuff inspires you, enjoy them, leverage them to create more wealth if that feels good but please don't associate your inner worth to them... you are priceless with or without that diamond ring, that multi-6-figure business, those box fresh kicks.

And so, I present The How NOT to Be Broke Manifesto

12 simple principles to bring you back to yourself, to your mission, to your values for financial freedom.

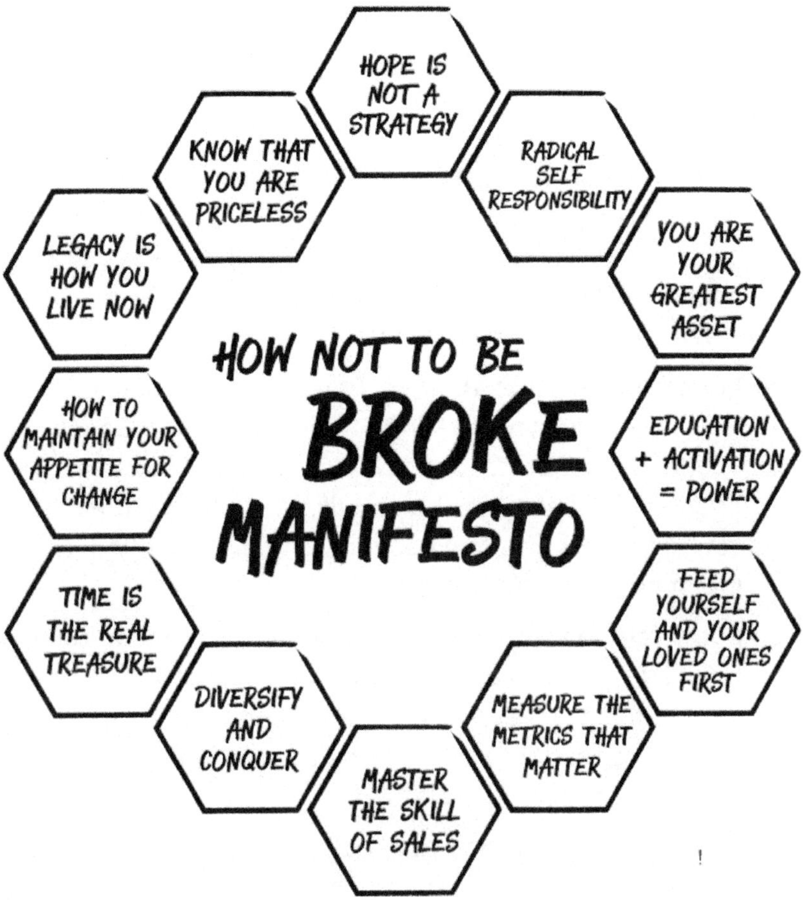


### How NOT to be Broke Manifesto

1. **Hope is NOT a strategy:** Hoping for financial stability is not the same as actively working towards it. Real financial security arises from planning, action, and perseverance. Instead of simply wishing for financial freedom, invest time in designing a realistic budget, saving consistently, and seeking investment opportunities.
2. **Radical Self Responsibility:** Your financial situation, whether positive or negative, is largely the outcome of the choices you

make. Embrace radical responsibility by acknowledging that your decisions impact your financial standing. Avoid blaming external factors or situations, and instead, seek solutions to improve.

3. **You are your Greatest Asset:** Recognise that investing in yourself can yield the greatest returns. This means prioritising personal development, mental and physical health, and continuous learning. When you are at your best, you can make the best financial decisions.
4. **Education + Activation = Power:** Knowledge is only a precursor for power. When combined with action, and intention though it becomes real power. Educate yourself on financial literacy, but also take steps to implement what you've learned. Reading about investing is one thing; actually investing is where the power lies.
5. **Feed yourself and your loved ones first:** Before indulging in luxuries or non-essentials, ensure that you've catered to your basic needs and those of your dependents. This means saving a portion of every income, ensuring health and well-being, and securing a safety net.
6. **Measure the metrics that matter:** Track your financial progress. This means monitoring your income, expenses, savings, and investments. Understanding these numbers provides clarity on your financial health and guides you in making informed choices.
7. **Master the skill of sales:** Whether you're selling a product, service, or yourself in a job interview, mastering the art of sales can open doors to numerous opportunities. This skill can bolster your income and offer a backup plan during financial downturns.
8. **Diversify and Conquer:** Relying on a single income stream or investment is a risky game. The more diverse your sources

of income and investments, the better protected you are from financial downturns. Just as nature thrives on biodiversity, your financial portfolio should thrive on a mix of assets. By spreading your resources across various opportunities, you reduce the risk of total loss and increase the potential for growth. Remember, don't put all your eggs in one basket; diversify them, and you're more likely to conquer financial instability.

9. **Time is the real treasure:** Understand that while money can be earned back, time cannot. Value your time. Spend it wisely, grab those short term wins often, but also invest in long-term growth, and ensure you are giving time to both professional and personal growth.
10. **Maintain your appetite for change:** The financial landscape and opportunities change with time. Stay adaptable. Continuously update your knowledge, be open to new financial tools or strategies, and don't be afraid to pivot when necessary.
11. **Legacy is how you live NOW:** The choices you make today shape the legacy you leave behind. Instead of waiting for "someday," act now. Live by the values, habits, and financial decisions you want to be remembered for.
12. **Know that you are priceless:** While it's essential to understand your financial worth, remember that your intrinsic value is immeasurable. You bring unique qualities, experiences, and insights to the world. Embrace this, and let it drive your actions and decisions.

### How NOT to be Broke Top Tip

Some ways to super charge these?

1. Download a copy of the manifesto from www.juliecreffield.com/broke and pin it somewhere you can see it each day

2. Write them out by hand in your current note book
3. Work through them...a quick read daily, a deep dive one a week, or one principle a month, the frequency doesn't matter., it is the repetition and the commitment to it as a tool that does.
4. Use them as mantras, write them on post it notes, share them in your socials
5. Use them as talking points with loved ones...they are relevant to so many other areas of life too

**Happy (adj.)**

late 14c., "lucky, favoured by fortune, being in advantageous circumstances, prosperous;" of events, "turning out well," from hap(n.) "chance, fortune". Sense of "very glad" first recorded late 14c. Meaning "greatly pleased and content" is from 1520s. Old English *eadia* (from ead "Wealth, riches") and *gesaelig,* which has become silly.

CHAPTER 13

# *KNOW THAT YOU ARE PRICELESS*

***While it's essential to understand your financial worth in terms of your day rate, or how you price your products and services...or maybe even knowing your net worth, your intrinsic value is immeasurable. You bring unique qualities, experiences, and insights to the world. Embrace this, and let it drive your actions and decisions.***

When I was 12-years-old, not long after meeting Uncle Les I acquired an old typewriter, I don't remember where it came from or even when it disappeared, which is reminiscent of many of the precious things I owned as a child.

It was a big old heavy thing, and it lived downstairs in the front room in our temporary accommodation in Walthamstow, being moved on and off the table where we ate, as there was no room in the bedroom which I shared with my 3 sisters.

We had been asked in English to write an autobiography and I was taking the assignment extremely seriously. I had begged my mum to buy me a replacement ribbon from WHSmith's which I am sure would been an expense she could have done without, and I had nabbed some white paper from the computer room at school...I was set to write a bestseller.

One of Six.

That was the title of the book.

I worked on that masterpiece every night after school for at least 2 weeks, and at the weekends when everyone else was playing outside. It told tales of my wider family, our good memories of childhood, and my hopes and aspirations for the future. I only mentioned briefly the challenges we were currently facing, ones that my teachers were all but aware of.

Handing it in, I am not sure I had ever been so proud of a piece of work... but more than that, I felt like finally someone was going to understand me, to see me, to see us... to see that not everyone has the same resources, but could still make the most of what they had. Still make something of themselves.

The final paragraph of One of Six read,

*"At the moment there is a lot going on in my life. We have moved house, completely out of the area we used to live, Christmas is coming and money is a precious thing, we are all thinking of ways to economise but still have fun.*

*I want to lead a long happy and full life. I want to be happy in work and have a happy family. I don't want to be rich I just want to be comfortable. That's all. That's all I want for the rest of my life"*

That's all.
That's all, I wanted.
It's all I have ever wanted.
But maybe it is NOT all I want now.

I found that book when I moved into my big old house in the countryside. I now have an office, a fit for purpose place for me to work from, rather than the corner of my front room where I had built my first two 6 figure businesses.

I have always kept old school books, and reports, and memorabilia of my life. I enjoy the nostalgia of it, but I am not sure I was expecting the emotional response that hit me upon finding that book in amongst the cardboard boxes I was unpacking.

Those sixteen A4 pages, which had turned a little yellow with age, despite being bound in a plastic cover with one of those long black slider things to hold it all together, those pages held so much emotion. They told so much of my early story, in my own simple words.

It immediately took me back to how I felt as a child, the dreams I had for my life but some kind of inner knowing that girls like me shouldn't want the things I do... I shouldn't expect them.

As I flicked through the document I found myself crying, no sobbing.

I think it was only in that moment, 6 months after moving into my million-pound barn conversion, that I realised how far I had come, how extraordinary my journey had been, the graft, the determination, the magic that had unfolded for me to have reached this point.

I had done all of this...little ole, (OK big ole) me.

It was quite overwhelming.

Almost like I couldn't breathe.

The photos stuck in with bluetac tipped me over the edge, autobiographies always have photos in the middle pages, right? These snapshots of me as a little girl, as a baby. One of me and my siblings with my Dad at Leigh on Sea eating cockles. One of me dressed as a witch (black bin bag and blue tights) for a school Halloween disco, me on the stage in one of my dancing school shows.

That little girl wanted so much to be seen, to be heard...she had so much to say. She wanted adventures, she wanted to travel, she wanted to laugh, and play, and swim in oceans in all corners of the globe.

Alongside the pencil ticks and spelling corrections were two comments from my English teacher at the time Miss Miller.

"It is very beautiful" in response to me saying I'd like to cycle around France one day, and "she sounds like a remarkable woman" when I described all the challenges my mum had faced overcoming cancer, and raising 6 kids alone.

It is very easy to romanticise your upbringing, and or to fill your head with stories that are only half true, one of the benefits of being a prolific diary keeper is I am able to look back and laugh at some of the things I said and quite strongly felt at the time, even if I know now with the benefit of become a parent that kids only know the half of it.

I have spent so much of my life trying to unpack those difficult feelings I had as a child and as a teenager, of not being good enough, not receiving enough love, enough praise... being in lack. Every life challenge, and disappointment amplifying those feelings of being broke... not being enough.

Perhaps much of my drive has been about proving people wrong, proving to myself perhaps that I am worthy.

I have worked with close to 20,000 women in the online space over the past decade through my various coaching programmes, and I can't tell you how many of them also feel like this, they are exhausted by the ups and downs of life, and the pursuit of health, wealth and happiness...and are constantly having to question whether they need "fixing".

I have held space for thousands of experienced and not so experienced business leaders in tears worrying about how they are going to cover their bills, frightened about the future, questioning their worth, questioning if they can ever achieve from their business the things they really want to.

It ALMOST always comes down to self-worth, self-belief, self actualisation.

As a business and life strategist it is my job to help people plot out and take action on the things they truly desire, and yet so many of them (even those playing at the highest of levels) still underestimate themselves, self-sabotage, under charge, over deliver, people please, and play small.

I think what my real job, what my real purpose is, on this planet, is to help other people see their intrinsic value. To help us all realise that we are not broken, and the things which have caused us pain in the past can actually help give us strength and a competitive edge now.

I needed to do that for me, to be able to do that for others... which makes the journey seem more than worth it now.

Creating financial safety and security for myself, especially since becoming a parent, a single parent at that, has often felt like banging my head against a brick wall. It has not been a straightforward story of incremental or even exponential growth.

I still have a way to go with this journey.

There is a tense tug of war between honouring my working-class roots, and the work ethic that comes with that, and then my desire for real freedom and challenging the idea of what someone like me should want... and more importantly what is even possible.

I work on that daily.

I am a business strategist
I am an author
I am a speaker
I am a visionary
I am a change maker
I am a facilitator of people

I am ideas generator
I am a grafter
I am brilliant at making money

You can do all of that too.

You can unlock your innate ability to leveraging the resources and assets you have at your disposal, but you have to understand your own worth.

You can use technological advances and the reach of social media to find clients and customers who share your world view, who need the transformation that your products and services lead to.

But that early conditioning, the stories that you have been told about wealth, and your own worth, they will bite you on the bum every time a lead goes quiet, every time a supplier screws you over, every time a social media post gets no likes... if you let it.

I share so much of my early life in this book, not just as a cutesy look back at my life (indulgent I know), but as a prompt for you to do the same. The things you cared about as a child, the things you wanted for yourself, they probably haven't changed much.

We come into this world perfect and pristine, bringing joy and hope to our families... the ultimate gift of abundance. Any yet over time we allow the outside world to strip away that feeling of being precious, and perfect, just as we are.

You can't ever "Charge your worth" ever.

There is no amount of money on the planet that quantifies your value.

Can you up your prices, learn not to overdeliver, improve your boundaries? 100%, but pay close attention to what you are making all that stuff mean. The online world is full of bullshit that picks at our core wounds, literally pulls those scabs off (urgh) with full abandon, day in day out causing us pain and discomfort, we have to protect ourselves from that daily... because it will break us otherwise.

## YOU ARE THE GOLD

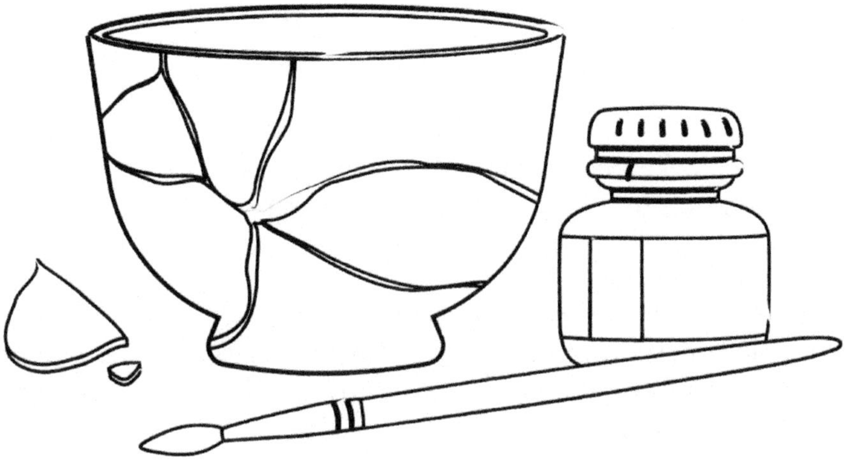

In the 500-year-old Japanese art of Kintsugi, which translates more or less as 'joining with gold', broken pottery is repaired with a glistening seam of lacquer and precious metal...symbolising the truth that nothing is ever truly broken.

The breakage is actually considered as beautiful and is treated as an important part of the object's history, the broken pot therefore is not just something to discard, but as something more precious than it was before.

How can you apply this principle to your life, to your business? How can stop constantly trying to hide the cracks, downplay the failures, instead wear them with pride.

When we allow others to see the beauty in our damaged imperfect selves (come on we are all slightly battered and bruised by life) we actually allow a better understand of the bigger picture of why you do what you do in the way that you do?

We don't need perfect leaders, we need transparent leaders, unafraid to share their vulnerabilities, to build empathy, to fully embrace the human experience in all its painful glory.

That's the gold!!!

Look.

I have built a life that I could only have dreamed of by simply being myself.... By embracing my wobbly bits, by letting people take me as I am, warts and all. That has become my super-power.

I am not a millionaire yet, and I am not even sure that is the goal, even if at times I have lived the lifestyle of one, but I have harnessed my ability to switch on the pipes of cashflow at will, which is always a useful skill in this day and age.

But fuck I've made it harder than it needed to be.

If only I had understood earlier in my life that making money wasn't just about working hard, being kind, and keeping my head down.

If only I had better understood the structures that keep us from truly succeeding, the inequality that still exists for many people when it comes to changing their circumstances.

If only I had realised earlier that even being your own boss comes with its own limitations... especially in terms of wealth creation, and that there are glass ceilings there too for many of us who choose that path.

But most importantly.

If only I had realised that being financially broke was a mindset, it was something I was often actively choosing, despite having many of the tools I needed to move into a more financially abundant state.

When you find yourself in lack, at rock bottom, or even just firmly in a financial rut, it is hard to be optimistic about the future. Instead of being brave and bold and taking the occasional risk which we know we must do as small business owners, instead we step back, we economise, we protect the resource we do have like our lives depend on it... because maybe they do.

Especially if we have been burned by investments or business relationships which went sour, as a result of relying too heavily on hope rather than robust strategy, business boundaries and a heavy dose of reality.

We deserve a seat at the table, we shouldn't even have to fight for it, in fact let's create our own mother fucking tables... it is what so many of us are having to do anyway... but let us not do this at any cost.

A whole bunch of wobbly broken chairs around the table doesn't really help anyone.

So one thing we can do for ourselves and for others is ensure our seats are as secure as possible for the journey, so that if and when we get there (wherever there is for you) we are fully resourced and not totally burned out and no good for anything.

Success is pointless if you are too knackered to enjoy it.

Finally.

I need you to understand that you have so many of the answers for unlocking wealth inside of you. The clues are totally in the broken bits the bits you feel are not palatable for the rest of the world, I assure you they are.

When we care less about what strangers on the internet think about us, and more about what we think about ourselves, something magical happens.

The way forward isn't "just" about making more money at any cost, that's the old skool, masculine way, and that has burnt us all out, and created a whole heap of stress and infighting among the folks who are willing to play in this space.

For me it's about creating safety and security first and foremost... financial safety and security, emotional safety and security, physical safety and security, spiritual safety and security.

Work on those things and you will be surprised at what can be achieved.

You are not BROKE, never were and never need to be again.

You are priceless.

You are the gold.

Don't EVER forget that.

Love Always

Julie

**How NOT to be Broke Top Tip**

Make a note in your diary for exactly a years time to...

1. Reread this book
2. Do the How Not to be Broke Audit again to look at progress
3. Complete the What Kind of Business am I REALLY running quiz
4. Review the metrics of success that matter to you
5. Get in touch and let me know how you have got on

# ACKNOWLEDGEMENTS

I feel like I have been painstakingly researching this book my whole life, even though in reality it took just 6 months and what feels like a billion hours to actually get it out of my head and onto paper, so it's a relief to have finally finished it.

It has been the most difficult piece of writing I have ever undertaken, as I process my thoughts and beliefs as I go...some of it challenging to my absolute core, revealing that I still have so much more learning and healing to do around allowing myself to receive.

When I first got the idea for the book I initially dismissed the concept because I didn't feel I had enough credibility to write a book on wealth, as in many ways I still felt a little broke myself...from recent events, but funnily enough stronger for having written the book.

But I figured if I felt like this given all of the wealth that I had amassed and the resources I had available to me to change my financial situation, then I was probably the best person to write it, and I saw it as an adventure, an experiment, rather than needing it to be a best seller.

I still fear the judgement though, as money is such an emotive topic, and we all carry such deep routed beliefs about worthiness and privilege. I also deeply feel the fear of being discredited by folks who benefit from the structures that keep the richest people rich and everyone else fighting it out on the bottom rungs of the ladder second guessing themselves.

I have a lot of people to thank for helping me get this book to print... -we never do it alone.

My family, although not the best at giving me practical or emotional support when things get tough, I love them regardless, and write this book as much for them as anyone. The stories I share about my upbringing and past generations are only my take on them... my Mum has often expressed her frustration at my account of our childhood, and I totally understand her reasons for that. My stories are of course my interpretation of my memories, and I wouldn't change my upbringing for a moment... it makes me who I am.

I would like to express my deepest gratitude to Selina Todd, for her life's work on helping us understand the struggle of the working class. The book Snakes and Ladders had a profound effect on me when doing research about social mobility, and her book Tastes of Honey was an absolute treat helping me to reconnect to one of my favourite jobs working as an usher at Joan Littlewoods Stratford East for £13 a shift as a theatre obsessed teenager.

My own education around money didn't really start until my mid-thirties and for that I deeply thank Denise Duffield Thomas for her books on money mindset, and also her incredible Money Bootcamp programme and online community that I have been part of for more than 7 years....that group keeps my in action with my money mindset, and shows me what is possible.

I must also give credit to Lisa Nichols who I spent 8 days in Mexico with, and Robert T.Kiyosaki, Pam Grout and Brene Brown for their amazing books on abundance, money and the human experience... check out www.juliecreffield.com/broke for a full reading list.

I have acquired an incredible network of cheerleaders over the last decade, and I will never forget the kindness of strangers off the internet. Every email and DM I receive cheering me on boosts my spirits and keeps me going.

I want to particularly thank my dear friends Bryony Thomas, Julie Holmes, Mel Sherwood, Vic O'Farrell, Stacy Moore, and Erin Chamberlain who have been there with me through the ups and the downs and never judged me regardless of where I am on that path.

I want to thank Erin for her support around the birth of this book, Helen Hill for the amazing graphics which she did for me with the tightest turn around, Josephine Elms for doing an incredible edit job for me, and for Amit for the layout and formatting... what are we on working in this way now, book number 4?

And also, to my two besties Nat & Tash, they have loved me and my "Tiny Tears' alter ego through every stage of my life, from back in the day when we would pool our money for vodka, until now, when nobody keeps tabs of who paid for the booze... there is just always an endless supply. I always feel incredibly rich in their company, and I never underestimate the power of uncontrollable laughter, unlimited Prosecco and 20+ years of friendship, to fill my cup.

I'd also like to thank my clients, especially the hardcore ones among you that have bought every book, signed up for every programme, supported me over the last 10 years on this weird and wonderful journey.

I think finally I would like to thank the people that have taught me the most valuable of lessons about wealth and worthiness... even if they hurt the most. We can't trust everyone, some people take advantage of your kindness, some do not have the capacity to create wins for anyone other than themselves.

My dad who left when I was 13, the various employers who made me redundant, the high profile coaches who have showed me how not to run an ethical business, the acquaintances who were nowhere to be seen when the shit really hit the fan, and the people who should have loved and supported me through various parts of my life whose bad behaviour or absence inevitably made me stronger and more resilient.

I now see these experiences as gifts.

Painful gifts, but gifts none the less.

The final thank you has to go to my beautiful daughter Rose. She drives so much of my work, my determination to break patterns, to do things different, to show her what is possible.

It can't be easy being my daughter... maybe one day you will write a book about what a nightmare it's been.

My money stuff is rubbing off on her though whether she likes it or not, "You deserve it mum" "What would your wealthy-self do?" and "There is always more" all phrases she repeats back to me frequently.

I am truly blessed.

There really is beauty to be found in the cracks.

If you have enjoyed this book please take a few minutes to leave me a review. Strangers off the internet buy books based on the recommendations of other strangers, isn't that incredible?

Some Authors have a budget to pay PR agencies, to pay for advertising, to take time away from their business to go on yearlong book tours... I don't have any of that (at the moment) but instead have a determination to get this book in the hands of 1 million Solopreneurs.

Will you help me do that?

## *OTHER BOOKS BY JULIE CREFFIELD*

Leading From the Back
Living a Bigger Life
Half Crazy
Scream if You Want to Run Faster
The Fat Girls Guide to Marathon Running
The Ultimate Fitness Planner
New Year, Same You
5 Weeks to 5K

**Coming Soon**

How Not to Be Broke Planner & Workbook
How Not to Be Broke...The Kids Edition

**Coaching Programmes By Julie**

- The How NOT to be Broke Sales Challenge
- The Year to Change® Your Life Mastermind
- The Solopreneur Success Roadmap
- The Legacy Masterplan Incubator

Find out more at www.juliecreffield.com

**Keynote Talks**

- How NOT to be broke...5 steps to financial freedom for solopreneurs
- From Lifestyle to Legacy...how to find the right business model for you
- From council estate to million-pound barn conversion...and almost back again
- The setting and achieving of BIG FAT STUPID GOALS

All media and speaking enquiries to julie@juliecreffield.com

Printed in Great Britain
by Amazon

28160987R00136